COOL careers for girls

for girls

in CONSTRUCTION

Also by the same authors

Cool Careers for Girls with Animals

Cool Careers for Girls in Computers

Cool Careers for Girls in Engineering

Cool Careers for Girls in Food

Cool Careers for Girls in Health

Cool Careers for Girls in Sports

IMPACT PUBLICATIONS

COOL careers for girls in CONSTRUCTION

CEEL PASTERNAK & LINDA THORNBURG

Copyright © 2000 by Ceel Pasternak & Linda Thornburg. All rights reserved. Printed in the United States of America. No part of this book may be used or reproduced in any manner whatsoever without written permission of the publisher: IMPACT PUBLICATIONS, 9104 Manassas Dr., Suite N, Manassas Park, VA 20111, Fax 703/335-9486.

Liability/Warranty: The authors and publisher have made every attempt to provide the reader with accurate information. However, given constant changes in the employment field, they make no claims that this information will remain accurate at the time of reading. Furthermore, this information is presented for information purposes only. The authors and publisher make no claims that using this information will guarantee the reader a job. The authors and publisher shall not be liable for any loss or damages incurred in the process of following the advice presented in this book.

Library of Congress Cataloging-in-Publication Data

Pasternak, Ceel, 1932-
   Cool careers for girls in construction / Ceel Pasternak & Linda Thornburg.
     p. cm.
   Includes bibliographical references (p.).
   Summary: Profiles ten women who work as nutritionists, personal trainers, doctors, dentists, or other health professionals and explains their duties and how they prepared for and got their positions.
   ISBN 1-57023-131-1 (soft)—ISBN 1-57023-135-4 (hc.)
   1. Building trades—Vocational guidance. 2. Vocational guidance for women.
3. Women construction workers. I. Thornburg, Linda, 1949- . II. Title.
TH159.P37 2000
                       624'.023—dc21

                           CIP

Publisher: For information on Impact Publications, including current and forthcoming publications, authors, press kits, bookstore, and submission requirements, visit Impact's Web site: www.impactpublications.com

Publicity/Rights: For information on publicity, author interviews, and subsidiary rights, contact the Public Relations and Marketing Department: Tel. 703/361-7300 or Fax 703/335-9486.

Sales/Distribution: All paperback bookstore sales are handled through Impact's trade distributor: National Book Network, 15200 NBN Way, Blue Ridge Summit, PA 17214, Tel. 1-800-462-6420. All other sales and distribution inquiries should be directed to the publisher: Sales Department, IMPACT PUBLICATIONS, 9104-N Manassas Dr., Manassas Park, VA 20111-5211, Tel. 703/361-7300, Fax 703/335-9486, or E-mail: coolcareers@impactpublications.com

Book design by Guenet Abraham
Desktopped by C. M. Grafik

*Dedicated to the women in
this book who were kind enough
to share their experiences with us in
order to help girls learn about
this rewarding work.*

Contents

Special Introduction by Connie Ashbrook, Executive Director, Oregon Tradeswomen Network, Portland, Oregon; former dump truck driver, carpenter, and elevator constructor.

IRONWORKER, APPRENTICE   5
☞ ...*The Iron Woman*

LANDSCAPE ARCHITECT, ENTREPRENEUR   13
☞ ...*The Outdoors Is Her Canvas*

ENTREPRENEUR   25
☞ ...*Her Company Focuses on Works in Progress*

ELECTRICIAN, JOURNEYMAN   35
☞ ...*High Voltage Work Gives Her Power*

HEAVY EQUIPMENT OPERATOR   43
☞ ...*She Shifts Gears to Build Highways*

MASTER PLUMBER   51
☞ ...*Plumb Perfect*

ELECTRICIAN, APPRENTICE   59
☞ ...*All the Right Connections*

CARPENTER, JOURNEYMAN 67
☞ ...*Crafting a Career She Loves*

SHEETMETAL WORKER, APPRENTICE 77
☞ ...*She Knows How the Air Flows*

ARCHITECT 85
☞ ...*She Plans Beautiful and Useful Buildings*

Getting Started On Your Own Career Path 99

What To Do Now

Recommended Reading

Training Centers, Trade Groups, and Construction Organizations

A Special Introduction by Connie Ashbrook

Executive Director, Oregon Tradeswomen Network, Portland, Oregon; former dump truck driver, carpenter, and elevator constructor.

I'll never forget the excitement of my first day building a bridge. Not that you could tell it was a bridge. It was basically a mud hole with tall pillars rising from it.

I was a brand-new apprentice carpenter, fresh from a 10-week pre-apprenticeship class where I learned the basics of using power tools, hammer, tape measure, and chalk line. I was partnered up with a journeyman—a more experienced worker who would teach me as we worked, and also keep me out of trouble. Joe was a little apprehensive, but also curious and amused at having "the girl" for his apprentice.

The term journeyman comes out of the guild systems of ancient Europe. Young people left their family home at around age 12 to become apprentices. Their families signed a contract with a master craftsperson who agreed to give the apprentices room and board, and teach them skills, in return for their labor. The contracts meant the apprentices were indentured and the master had the right to tell the apprentices what to do. The master had several journeymen working for him who would train the new apprentices under his supervision. Once the apprentices were fully trained, they took an exam and produced examples of their craft to become journeymen. They were then free of their indenture and could travel—journey—and work with different masters until they earned enough to set themselves up as masters.

This system, modified for modern times, and these terms have come down to us today. Apprentices still sign a contract of indenture agreeing to work and learn. Apprentices are still paired up with journeymen who teach them their skills as they do the job. Employers (no longer called masters) still agree to see that apprentices are trained in return for their labor—but instead of room and board, apprentices receive a wage that increases as their knowledge and usefulness to their employer increases.

To get back to my bridge building experience, why was Joe so curious about "the girl"? When I started as a carpenter in 1977, the trades were just opening to women. Most of the 50 men who were building the bridge with me as laborers, heavy equipment operators, ironworkers, cement masons, and carpenters had never worked with a woman before. For several months (before Maureen, a cement mason, started) I was the only woman working on the project.

I had been working as a waitress since I graduated from high school and had never worked around so many men before. We learned a lot from each other. I learned carpentry skills, and the men learned that a woman could be strong, capable, and a good carpenter. Waitressing is physical work, but not nearly as physical as carpentry. The first 2 months, I would go home and lie on the couch after work because I was so tired and sore. My arms would be numb from lifting, hammering, and sawing. But I got used to it. I took a lot of pride in my strength. Construction work isn't just physical, though. You need to have a love of problem solving and of using your brain, tools, and materials to make things happen. Teamwork is also really important because the work of each craft—carpenter, ironworker, cement mason, and others—all becomes part of a greater whole. I became part of a team of workers, who together changed a mud hole into a beautiful, curving bridge.

Now women are about 2.8% of the construction workforce in the United States. Most men have worked with strong, capable women and so are not surprised or astonished to have a woman for their co-worker. There are still some "old-hands" who want to see women back in the kitchen, and some young punks who resent women because they feel their masculinity is threatened by a woman's competence in their trade. Most men are like Joe toward women in the trades—willing to accept, to train, and to enjoy a woman as a co-worker and fellow human being.

The variety of construction work, the interesting and challenging jobs related to it, and the high pay and benefits all make trades and construction careers great choices that you might pick for your future. In this book, you will read what women working in the trades and in other construction-related jobs have to say about their work. You will read the stories of women who are ironworkers, electricians, architects, and construction managers.

Several times a year, I drive over the bridge I helped build, picking up family and friends from the airport. Every time I feel a sense of pride that my labor built this beautiful, useful, enduring structure. "Look," I say to them, "I built this bridge!"

Getting Started Now

This book is a great place to start researching careers in construction. The stories of the women in this book will give you a good idea of the educational requirements, a typical day, and the challenges and rewards of the many different kinds of careers that they have chosen. You will also learn that some women made their career choices when they were girls. Along with each story, you will find a checklist with some clues about what type of personality would be suitable for a particular job. Information about salaries and employment opportunities is also provided. The last chapter, Getting Started on Your Own Career Path, gives you advice about what to do now and identifies some helpful organizations you may contact for additional information.

COOL careers for girls in CONSTRUCTION

Colleen Lynch

Ironworker Apprentice, Northwest Ironworkers Union, Local 29, Portland, OR

Ironworker Apprentice

The Iron Woman

Colleen Lynch grew up a rough and tumble tomboy who loved things like jumping off roofs and playing baseball and football with the boys. Her family—father, stay-at-home mother, three sisters, and a brother—lived in the Bay area of California. "My father owned a steel fabricating shop, and if we didn't get good grades in school, we had to work weekends in his shop." Colleen was good in math, but from age 14 to 18 she spent many weekends working in her dad's shop.

"The steel comes in 60 foot long bars. I learned a lot about preparing the steel to be used to reinforce concrete. We'd cut it and bend it into the various shapes using pretty heavy duty hydraulic equipment. In the sum-

IRONWORKER: Apprentice gets 65% of scale (journeyman basic wage is $25 per hour) for working and passing the training classes. Contractors can pay more if they wish. Workers get health benefits and a pension annuity, but no vacation pay.

COLLEEN'S CAREER PATH

- A tomboy, likes math
- Works in dad's shop
- Graduates high school, works retail

mertime, we'd get out of the shop and work at the building sites. It gave me a good taste for what the work was like."

After high school graduation, Colleen held a variety of jobs. She took a job as an apartment building manager (a free apartment goes along with the job), which she enjoyed because she has lots of energy and the job was more physical than office work. But when

Women can do anything. We may not be as strong physically, but you don't need to be.

some computer courses and had office jobs—many of them in construction offices. "I liked working with construction people—the dress was casual and the atmosphere laid back."

Colleen married, had a daughter, Adriana, and moved to Portland. To be able to work and stay home with Adriana, Colleen, now divorced, took a her daughter turned four and could attend school, Colleen looked for a better paying job so she could send her daughter to private school.

Colleen started working with her brother-in-law, a contractor, and getting information about the trades. "I talked to people on the job sites—plumbers, electricians, carpenters—

 Takes computer courses, works in construction offices

 Marries, has daughter

 Moves to Portland

and asked about their apprentice programs. I chose the ironworker program for several reasons. One, they didn't have night or Saturday classes, which would have been hard for me, having to care for my daughter. The training was day classes during one month in the winter. Two, the program was four years, not five. Three, I had experience in rebar (reinforcing concrete with steel bars) and I wanted to learn how to do welding."

Colleen went down to the union hall and asked if there were any openings in the Ironworkers Union's apprentice program. "Luckily for me, they wanted to hire females and they had openings. I took a written test, then had an interview with two people—one was the contractor who later hired me." Colleen became an apprentice with and still works for the contractor, Carr Construction.

Enjoys the Environments, the Challenges

Colleen, now in her third year as an apprentice, has enjoyed learning the ironworker trade. She's had classes

COLLEEN'S CAREER PATH

▼ Works as apartment building manager

▼ Becomes ironworker apprentice

in rigging, welding, and working with ornamental steel (hand rails, ornamental wrought iron). She's also enjoyed the good wages and the benefits the Northwest Ironworkers Union provides—health care, a pension annuity, and a hiring hall for getting work.

"What I like best about the work is working outside and the freedom to be working independently. No one is looking over my shoulder. I love the challenges and going to different worksites—not seeing the same four walls like I did in office work."

On a typical day, Colleen gets up at 4:30 a.m. She makes coffee, cleans up her dinner dishes, and makes lunches for herself and Adriana. She listens to the weather report to decide what to wear. Colleen often wears layers so she can take off a shirt later in the day when it warms up. Before she leaves for work, she walks her half-asleep daughter to her neighbor, who later will feed her breakfast and take her to school. When Colleen gets off work in the early afternoon, she will pick up her neighbor's daughter and Adriana and bring them to her home. "There are a lot of single moms living in this area and we help each other out."

Colleen checks in at the work site by 6:30 a.m. There is usually a meeting to let everyone know how the work is going and to deliver a brief safety reminder. Then Colleen collects her gear and whatever tools she'll need. She usually works with a partner, partly for safety reasons, although "welding is a solitary activity. It's not social. You wear leather gloves, fireproof 'sleeves' to protect your clothes, and you're sort of alone inside the welder's hood. I'm sure more tolerant of heat now than I used to be."

From Bottom Slabs to Red Iron

Colleen does both major types of iron work—"rebar" and structural. The rebar is working with the iron bars that reinforce concrete sections of buildings and bridges. The structural is working with the "Big Iron," metal I-beams (so named because they look

CAREER CHECKLIST ✓

You'll like this job if you ...

- Are not afraid of heights

- Don't mind getting dirty and greasy

- Like working outside

- Like to keep physically fit

- Have confidence in yourself, won't be intimidated

- Are not sensitive, won't get your feelings hurt when men comment or criticize

- Have a sense of humor

like the capital letter I) that form the frames of buildings.

One of the first construction steps when starting a new building is laying down the foundation, the bottom slab. Before the concrete is poured, the ironworkers create a mat of iron bars. The big pillars that rise up and the walls also have the bars. Sometimes, the mat for a wall is created on the ground, the concrete is poured, dries, and then the wall is lifted up into place with cranes. This is called "tilt-up." Other times, the ironworkers climb the wall, carrying the rods on their knees. Then, they tie them in place.

Big cranes are a part of the scene when the work involves the long and heavy I-beams. They help lift and move beams into place. One of the first parts of an apprentice's training is to learn to rig the iron so the crane can move it safely. Colleen had to use her math skills to do this. "You have to figure the weight, size, and shape of the load, even if it's just one I-beam. You have to know the center so it will balance. Then you learn how to rig it with chokers (nylon and wire straps) and where to attach the cables."

As the skeleton of the building goes up, Colleen will be rigging the I-beams, choosing the correct pieces for the crane to lift. The people at the top will catch them and bolt them into place. Then Colleen and others will climb up and do what they call "plumb up"—complete the bolting process, adjusting to be sure the frame is level and welding corner joints and other places where bolts are not enough, where more strength is needed. "The welding is like the glue that holds things together."

Colleen also has worked on highway ramps and bridges. "The big piers (the columns that hold up the ramps) and the bridges are loaded with rebar. Some columns start small as they come out of the ground and then get wider and bigger as they go up."

While a lot of Colleen's time away from the job is spent sharing child care with her neighbors, she does take some leisure time to go camping with her friends. She also enjoys books and television programs about how historic buildings were built.

The most important thing is to show up and be consistent in my work.

Catherine Mahan

Owner, Mahan Rykiel Associates, Baltimore, MD

Major, Fine Arts; Master's in Landscape Architecture

Landscape Architect, Entrepreneur

The Outdoors Is Her Canvas

As a girl growing up just outside Boston, Catherine Mahan loved the outdoors, and she liked to paint and draw. These days, she frequently works outside and gets to use her design skills in creating landscapes. Catherine is a landscape architect who owns her own business in Baltimore, Maryland.

One of Catherine's most challenging projects right now is the design of a little island that county officials in Virginia want to turn into a park. A 12-lane bridge will be built over the island to connect Maryland to Virginia. The county wants to put a foot and bicycle path and park above the bridge to connect the island's two sides—it will be a bridge above a bridge.

LANDSCAPE ARCHITECT: Low to mid $20,000s to start, up to $40,000 to $60,000 for senior designer. State registration is required in most states.

ENTREPRENEUR: People who start their own business may not earn any salary in the beginning. They invest their own money in the business, they get more money through loans or venture capital, and, until they make a profit or "go public" by selling stock, they probably pay themselves a small salary and put profits back into the business to help it grow.

CATHERINE'S CAREER PATH

▼ Travels to Europe, loves languages, art      ▼ Graduates college, teaches, works in art gallery      ▼ Gets master's degree in landscape architecture

Catherine will design ways to build a path that will get people from an elevation of 10 feet on the island to 80 feet (the top of the foot and bicycle path) without creating too steep a slope. If the slope is too steep, the path won't be accessible for people pushing baby strollers or those in wheelchairs.

She has to consider what type of material to use for the path and how to fill in the island when dirt is taken out to build the path, figure out how to best protect the wetlands in that area, create the recreation areas in the park by using space effectively, and choose the right plantings for the island. Because the soil will only be three feet deep at the top, this alone is a difficult challenge. Large plants that require deep roots can't be used on top of the path. Catherine also has to consider the amount of wind and sun that will reach the top of the path when she chooses plants.

As the owner of Mahan Rykiel Associates, Catherine works on many landscape design projects for city, county, state, and federal government. Catherine developed this "niche" for her business by becoming certified as a woman-owned business. Governments often have requirements that a certain amount of construction money go to businesses that are minority or woman-owned. Because her company could do the work well, she gained a reputation with government clients. Her company has worked on landscape design for commuter train stations (including parking lots and neighborhoods along the line that runs throughout the Delaware Valley); for Camden Yard where the Orioles

 Works as state park planner, marries John

 Joins landscape firm, travels, designs commercial sites

 Has son, starts own business

baseball team plays; and for the Baltimore Aquarium.

Catherine and her 25 employees also design landscapes for shopping centers, retirement centers, and other commercial projects, as well as for large houses. "We might have a homeowner who is hiring an architect to build a big house. We would work with the architect on locating where the house would go on the land, how the driveway should be laid out to make best use of the space, how the land would be graded to save as many trees as possible, and how to face the house so that you could have outdoor spaces that get as much sun as possible. Often with these projects, we'll do fences, terraces, gardens, play areas, swimming pools, and maybe some orchards or meadows. We'll grade the surface of the land, but if it involves systems underground, we will work with an engineer to design that part of it."

Credit: Charles Herbert, Image C Photography

CATHERINE'S CAREER PATH

Has daughter,
▼ business certified
as woman-owned

Gets partner,
▼ business goes
international

Starts Her Own Company

Catherine started her own company in 1983. Her first child, her son, Wilson, was two years old and she found it hard to manage working at a job with a 45-minute commute. Besides, the architects at the landscape architecture company where she was working gave her a hard time when she had to call in to take time off if her son was sick. "I needed to change jobs, but at that point, I thought, if I do this again, I'm going to do it for myself instead of promoting somebody else's career."

Catherine is married to John W. Hill, the former Dean of the Architecture School at the University of Maryland. One of his former students, Robert Goldman, a practicing architect, offered to let her use some space in his own office to get her business started.

Catherine was designing the landscaping for a shopping center in West Virginia at the time she decided to leave the firm. The partners there let her take the customer with her when she left her job—first, to help her get started, and second, because she was the only one who really knew anything about the project. She was working to design the interior plantings for the center—big courtyards and waterfalls and palm trees. The project had undergone some big changes, and the landscaping had to be redesigned several times.

"I thought about how I was going to get some more work when I finished the shopping center. I put together a slide show of projects that I had done in my previous jobs, and I just started calling architects and other design firms in the downtown Baltimore area. It turned out that a lot of landscape architects were located in the suburbs, and there was nobody really downtown where all the architecture firms were. Anybody that I could get to look at my work, I did. I said 'I will do whatever you need.' The architecture community made up my clients. Most of the projects I was interested in had a building component. The client would hire the architect and expect him or her to hire the engineer and the landscape architect. People started calling me because they knew that I could get the project done fast, where if they called a big landscape architectural firm, they would have to wait a month or so."

Catherine was grateful to Robert for his offer of office space. She was able to use his telephone and copying machine, and she didn't have to pay any rent at the beginning. When she built up her own customer base, she moved to another office in the same building and began paying all her own expenses.

CAREER CHECKLIST ✓

You'll like this job if you ...

- Like art and can see how things fit together to create a pleasing image

- Can communicate well in writing, speaking, and graphically

- Like to work in a team environment

- Want to make outdoor and/or indoor spaces beautiful

- Like trees, plants and working with the land

"After I had been in business for several years and had a couple of employees, I realized there were specific programs to foster women's businesses. I got certified as a woman's business enterprise. Then I started getting work from the Maryland Department of Transportation, and the reputation of our company began to grow. This is the way these minority programs are supposed to work. You may have an advantage in getting the work, but you don't keep those clients or get new ones unless you can really deliver."

When Catherine's company was 10 years old, and she had about 10 people working for her, she realized that she was exhausted with making every decision, even down to what type of paper clips to buy. A man she had previously worked with wanted to leave his job. Because she had worked with him in the past and knew they had similar philosophies about landscape architecture, she asked if he wanted to

Some of our competitors think we get handouts because we are certified as a minority business, but we work darn hard for the work we have.

come to work with her and share the responsibility for some of the decisions. He did, and he brought a number of international clients with him. Now Catherine's firm does work all over the world. The firm continues to grow and Catherine gets to devote more time to developing the clients she is most interested in—college campuses and retirement communities on the East Coast of the United States. "I love to travel overseas, but not for business."

A Love for the Fine Arts

Catherine didn't think about landscape architecture as a career until she had been out of college for more than five years. She attended Georgetown University in Washington, D.C., because it had a good language school. She had spent the summer after high school in England and France and was interested in studying romance languages. But she found the language program too dry and technical for her taste. "I majored in French. After my sophomore year I had taken all my electives and the Georgetown program was very linguistics oriented. I hadn't realized that as a high school student. I was more interested in art, culture, music, and literature. I wanted to transfer to the fine arts program at Georgetown because I wasn't being challenged enough. But it was the early 1970s, and at that point, women were not allowed into the School of Arts and Sciences. You could go to the Language Institute, the School for Foreign Service, or the Nursing School, but arts and sciences were really only for men. I was struggling with what to do, when the school decided to let women into arts and sciences. They admitted six women that year—my roommate and I and four other women got in. I had these classes with 200 men and me, so asking questions was somewhat intimidating. It was strange but it was also fun. We were rebels on the cutting edge. Besides, I was back doing the things I loved—painting, drawing, and print-making."

Catherine graduated with a degree in fine arts, but ended up taking a job

as a language teacher anyway. "There weren't any jobs for painters advertised in the paper, except house painters. Teaching language was my day job for five years. I was fairly good at it, and it allowed me to pay the rent. But eventually, I left it because it really wasn't all consuming. I began working in an art gallery and taking some painting classes at the Corcoran Museum."

How She Decides on Landscape Architecture

"I was trying to figure out what really was going to be my life's work and how I could make a career out of work that I loved. The art gallery I worked in had little business, so I used to sit and look out the windows of the gallery into a plant store across the street. There was a guy working upstairs who didn't have much to do either, and he would come into the gallery and talk to me. One night I went to see a movie called *Alfredo, Alfredo*. The lead character was this Italian American woman. She was bright and warm and happy and you just looked at her and said, 'this is the person I would like to be.' Someone in the movie asked her what she did, and she said 'I'm a landscape architect.' I thought, 'I want to be like her.' But it wasn't as far out as it seemed at the time. I had an uncle who was a professor of landscape architecture at Harvard, and he was kind of a household word when I was growing up. I heard 'Uncle Walter said pitch the terrace that way so it will drain,' and things like that when I was a girl.

"The day after I saw the movie, I went back to work and asked the guy from upstairs, who worked in education, to see what he could find out about landscape architecture for me. He came back with a printout of all the schools in the country, degrees they offered, and their course requirements. I was pretty tied to the Washington area because I had lots of friends there, so I applied and was admitted to the University of Virginia in Charlottesville, which had a master's program for people who hadn't studied landscape architecture in undergraduate school."

phy. That's one of the fun things about landscape architecture; it's rarely anyone's first career. During a summer program we did simple drafting and lettering and learned the conventions of architectural drawings. We did a little bit of land surveying, a little bit of plant materials, and what you needed to know about the land for drainage and design. By the time we started in the fall, everybody had the basics. It was clear to me that we were

> My dad had started his own business. Even though I hadn't thought that I would be in that position, I could model myself after him when the time came.

The landscape architecture program at UVA was designed for people who had all sorts of backgrounds. "We had people from fine arts, environmental sciences, biology, and philoso-

doing design work, but we were also doing a lot of problem solving, which I thought was the really interesting side. How can we get the water to run down hill so that it is away from the

GROUNDBREAKERS

A Founding Member and "Gardener"

Landscape architecture is one of the most diversified of the design professions. Landscape architects design the environment around buildings in neighborhoods, towns, and cities. They also protect and manage the natural environment, from forests and fields to rivers and coasts.

The American Society of Landscape Architects was founded in 1899. One of its founding members is Beatrix Farrand (1872-1959). A landscape architect trained at the Arnold Arboretum in Massachusetts, she called herself a "landscape gardener." She is known for her work on the Yale University quadrangles and the grounds of Dumbarton Oaks in Washington, DC.

Beatrix was influenced by Gertrude Jekyll (1843-1933), an English painter who took up gardening at age 47. Jekyll introduced the herbaceous border to gardens and favored a volume of plantings, blending colors of flowers, foliage, and bark.

Source: American Society of Landscape Architects and National Women's History Project, Windsor, CA

---

house, and how can we save the trees and also build the baseball diamond? It was a fun challenge, and the fact that I was still doing drawing and design was really great. I was so happy. Three afternoons a week I had a studio course from 12 to 5 where I worked on design problems. The core courses were things like plants of the region, geology, ecology, planting design, construction, road design, and a little bit of the behavioral sciences."

Her First Job

While she was in graduate school, Catherine met her future husband, who was an architect. When she graduated, she decided to move to Baltimore, near where he lived, and landed a job with the state's Department of Natural Resources, working as a park planner. "It was good experience but it wasn't fabulously exciting. Mostly I wrote programs for the parks. For example, they would say, 'we've developed a new camping area in this park, and it needs to have 14 bathrooms and three drinking fountains.' I would tell them where to put them. Then, outside consultants would do the work."

On her next job, Catherine got lots of experience doing commercial work for an architecture firm that had some in-house landscape architects. Her company flew her to different areas of the country, where she did site inspections, talked to contractors, and obtained materials for the landscape design. When that company, RTKL, bought another landscape architect firm, Catherine got transferred to a new location, where the people didn't know her. That was the job she left to start her own company.

Catherine has two children—a 13-year-old daughter and an 18-year-old son who is just starting college. "Like his mother at his age, he doesn't know what he wants to do with his life yet. We're late bloomers," she says.

Christine Keville

President and Owner, Keville Enterprises, Inc., Marshfield, MA

Major in mathematics, minor in computer science
Master's in Engineering—Construction Management,
Certificate in Construction Inspection

Entrepreneur

Her Company Focuses on Works in Progress

In 1991, Christine Keville decided she had gone just about as far as she could go in the construction industry as an employee in someone else's company. With her construction management master's degree and life's savings, she struck out on her own. Today she is the owner and president of a construction management company in Marshfield, Massachusetts, that employs 60 people throughout the country and in Puerto Rico.

Christine's company, Keville Enterprises, Inc. (KEI), manages various aspects of many large construction projects. She and her employees (construction managers and engineers, project managers, inspectors, lawyers, and computer specialists) have worked on bridges, tunnels, railroads, high-

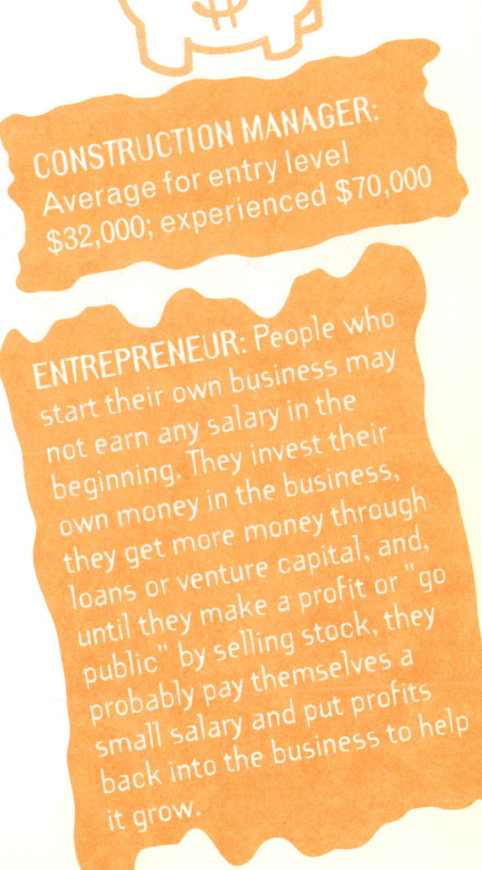

CONSTRUCTION MANAGER: Average for entry level $32,000; experienced $70,000

ENTREPRENEUR: People who start their own business may not earn any salary in the beginning. They invest their own money in the business, they get more money through loans or venture capital, and, until they make a profit or "go public" by selling stock, they probably pay themselves a small salary and put profits back into the business to help it grow.

CHRISTINE'S CAREER PATH

- Builds highways in her yard, visits job sites with dad
- Works summers at construction jobs, graduates from college
- Works as office manager in the industry

ways, waterfronts, and airports. KEI sometimes works as a subcontractor or subconsultant on multi-million dollar projects. At other times her company will get a contract from a regional or national government agency to oversee various parts of the construction job. For example, Christine's company was responsible for inspecting construction to assure work was performed according to contract requirements for a base owned by the U.S. Coast Guard in San Juan, Puerto Rico. People from Christine's company documented the daily work activities and monitored the progress of the work to make sure it was per-

It's rewarding whether you are involved in heavy/highway construction, airport, transit, or building construction projects.

formed according to specifications and that it was completed within the time frames specified in the contract.

Another KEI project was to oversee the work on a contract to relocate various pipelines for Sunoco at Philadelphia International Airport. Christine's company had to make sure all of the work was performed in accor-

 Establishes trust fund

 Gets master's degree

Opens own company, takes photos

dance with contract documents and to verify that work met the requirements of the established criteria and applicable codes and/or standards.

One of the largest projects KEI is involved in is Boston's Central Artery/Third Harbor Tunnel Project, it is otherwise known at the CA/T project. This project is the largest, most complex and technically challenging highway project in the history of the United States. It is a $10.8 billion, multimodal transportation project unlike anything ever attempted in a U.S. city. KEI is providing welding and

metals inspection services, electrical inspection services, and contract administration support, specializing in contractor claims and scheduling services.

As head of KEI, Christine's typical day consists of going to the gym for an early morning workout, then getting to work by 7:30 a.m. She may write proposals for new work, negotiate contracts, contact clients about ongoing work, interview prospective employees, or pursue working as a contract team with other companies. She could be forecasting what the company will need

CHRISTINE'S CAREER PATH

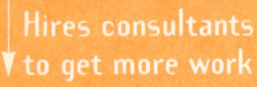 Hires consultants to get more work

 Expands KEI, hiring full-time employees

to do in the future, reviewing cost and scheduling on current projects, or she could go to job site meetings. She also might attend professional society luncheons or dinners to network and get information, or attend a board meeting for one of the boards of directors on which she serves.

A Curiosity and Love for Construction

Christine was exposed to the construction industry from an early age. Her father, who became a top construction industry leader, was a surveyor who went to night school for eight years to get the skills he needed. After he became a construction manager, he would sometimes take Christine and her sisters with him on weekends when he went to inspect transportation projects in the Boston area. They went down the vent shafts at construction sites. Early on, Christine developed a curiosity and love of the construction industry. Her father would bring home blocks of wood, and she and her friend Scotty would spend hours in the backyard, constructing their newest version of the next superhighway. Today Scotty also is employed in the construction industry.

Christine loved gymnastics and was lucky to have a mother who would take her to the gym five days a week to work out three hours a day. She loved the competitive nature of the sport, and also the fact that it required teamwork to be able to compete. Her team got to travel to Europe and throughout the United States for competitions. She enjoyed her grammar school and high school years and established many good friendships.

At her college, North Adams State, she majored in mathematics, was president of her class, and pledge master and treasurer of the *Pi Upsilon Omega* sorority. She lived with 12 girls in a house off campus. Christine and many of her roommates from college still maintain the great relationships that they shared throughout their college years.

During summers and on winter breaks from college, Christine worked as a union laborer for a major general contracting company. This work was sometimes demanding and strenuous, but it taught her "from the ground up" how projects were built. "It was a great learning process. It gave me a true respect for all aspects and elements of construction."

When she graduated from college, Christine found a job as an office manager for another major general contracting company. She stayed with that company for six and one-half years before venturing out on her own. Christine worked on different

CAREER CHECKLIST ✓

You'll like this job if you ...

- Are determined and strong willed
- Are open minded
- Are organized
- Are a good listener and communicator
- Are very much a team player

types of projects and learned from seasoned veterans. The vice president of the general construction company asked her if she would like to return to school to study construction. She immediately took him up on his offer. She enrolled in a few construction-related courses, and then entered Northeastern University for their master's program in construction management. Christine worked during the day and attended school at night. It made for a long day, but the people she came into contact with were interesting, and the course work was challenging and rewarding.

Just before she graduated from college, Christine's father, who had cancer, passed away. It was a difficult time for her, but she considered herself lucky to have known her dad, who touched so many lives in such positive ways. Her dad had been a tremendous

Work is always exciting. It is fast paced because you have to keep projects on track and under budget.

role model for her and was always supportive of her career. Christine considers her greatest accomplishment the creation of a trust fund in honor of her father. The Francis Keville Trust Fund was initially established to contribute to the Jordan Hospital Radiation Center and to distribute scholarships to high school and college students. Over the years, the events held to raise money became so successful that the trust fund raised enough for the hospital to name the radiation center at Jordan Hospital in memory of Christine's dad. "There was never a day in my life where I felt so fulfilled as when that happened," she says. Christine is now an active board member of the hospital. The trust fund is in its 11th year and continues to contribute to cancer research, scholarships, and numerous charitable organizations.

Research Leads to Photography Service

After working in the industry for nine years, Christine saw that the only way to reach the top of a construction management and engineering company was to create the company herself. Although the industry was changing in terms of the opportunities available for women, it wasn't changing fast enough to suit Christine. But to open her own company, she needed to answer many questions. For example, what type of services should she offer and where would she acquire the necessary financing to start her company? As part of her research, Christine talked to many industry professionals about what was needed in the industry.

What sort of a niche would she be able to fill? As she was doing her research she thought about what would be feasible to do, given the economic climate at the time. It was 1991, there was a recession, and loans were hard to acquire.

One day, she was sitting in an office trailer at a construction job site, when the supervisor came in and started looking at photos that had been taken to document the progress of the job. He said he wished that construction photographers knew more about construction. Many of the photos weren't useful because they were pictures of things that didn't really matter, like stock piles of materials. The photographer had missed some important parts of the project. Christine had a special knack for photography, but she had never thought of making a living at it. She thought this would be a good way to start her own business—offering photography services to document the progress of construction jobs. She enrolled in a six-week photography course and gave her employer notice. She was able to invest in some high-quality cameras and other equipment because she had saved some money.

This idea launched Christine's company. People began hiring her to take construction photographs or to record work on video. She still lived at home with her mother, and she had a generous boyfriend, so her living expenses were minimal. She invested every cent she made back into the business. No job was too large or too small for Christine.

One day someone asked her if she did aerial photography and without giving it a second thought she said yes. She had never even seen the inside of a helicopter. But she rented a helicopter and a pilot, took off the doors, strapped herself in, and went up and took photographs. Then Christine was able to add aerial photography to the growing list of services KEI offered.

Christine's company was growing, and she was doing more than just taking pictures. When she got an opportunity to bid on construction services, she took it. If she needed help, she hired a consultant. These consultants, who were experienced construction professional engineers, charged her large sums of money. But she considered them teachers and learned everything she could from them. Christine put in 14 hours or more a day, building her business. She had to do the labor, the marketing, the contracting with consultants, and everything else a small business requires. Her sister, who is now a full-time employee, helped on the weekends with the accounting.

Christine often took a change of clothes with her so that she could work in the field in the morning and meet with a client in the afternoon. "I felt like Superman looking for a telephone booth to change clothes in," she says. "I got to know where every McDonalds in the state was."

The Big Break

Hard work and perseverance were making Keville Enterprises well known in the construction and transportation industries. Although KEI was successfully tackling many different types of projects, Christine's really big break came on the Central Artery/Tunnel project in Boston. Christine and another inspection firm put together a first rate inspection team and a top notch proposal as a joint venture. Five years ago they got a welding and metals inspection services contract. Today KEI also performs other inspection and contract administration services on this multi-million dollar project. The project is at 100 percent design and 50 percent construction completion. "The engineering applications and construction innovations will transform Boston into the premier city of the United States," Christine says.

Christine devotes her spare time to her family and friends and to running the trust fund in honor of her father. She also serves on the boards of many national construction organizations and transportation organizations, including the Construction Management Association of America, where she recently was chairperson for their national conference.

33

Julie Odendahl

Commercial, Industrial Inside Wireman, Journeyman, International Brotherhood of Electrical Workers, Local 110, St. Paul, MN

Electrician, Journeyman

High Voltage Work Gives Her Power

"It was the most intricate arrangement I'd ever seen," says Julie Odendahl about a difficult job she recently completed at a new elementary school. "Most of the lighting was run by remote relays that allowed half the lights to stay on until 9:00 at night and the other half to go off at 5:00 p.m. to save energy. Then there are motion detectors that shut lights off in rooms that are unoccupied. Sometimes I had seven or eight wires all on the same circuit. I had to keep track of the wires I needed for the motion sensors, for the relays, for the actual lighting, and for the power switch. My boss knew I could handle it all, so he pretty much left me alone. When we fired everything up, the only areas that didn't work were the ones I wasn't working

ELECTRICIAN: Regular contractor employer pays union scale wage, $24.71 per hour for journeyman; apprentice starts at 50% of that wage, and gets increase every six months with good performance. Overtime is work more than 40 hours a week and pays double time on Saturday and Sunday (for example, $12 per hour plus $12 = $24 per hour). The contractor contributes to the health plan and pension plan set up by the union. By the time you have finished your four-year apprenticeship, you are eligible for up to three weeks vacation time. How much you get is based on how many hours you have worked.

JULIE'S CAREER PATH

Gets first job at bakery, graduates high school  Works at electronics firm  Strips tobacco

on. It was pretty cool that he trusted me so completely."

It's been a long road to reach the point at which Julie's bosses display so much trust. Part of the reason she inspires trust today is her self-confidence. "I almost quit this profession a few years back. There was one guy who would follow me around everywhere, checking up on me all the time. Finally, I thought to myself, 'I've been counseling women in the construction trade for six years now not to take this kind of stuff, and here I am taking it.' So I took off for the Black Hills of South Dakota and ended up on the coast of Oregon, visiting a friend for a couple of months. The turning point was when I got back. I knew what I was going to take and what I wasn't, and ever since, things have been great. I've worked for some great people and I've been doing really well. In the last four years, I've gotten to the point where I'm confident in my ability, and the guys are starting to say, 'she knows what she's doing.' I love going to work in the morning."

Julie loves the work because it's both mentally and physically challeng-

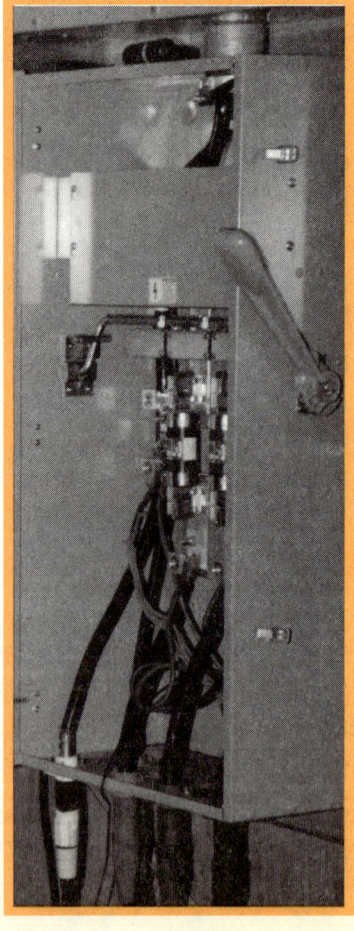

 Works as cook

 Gets first job as electrician's helper

 Enters St. Paul's Technical Institute then Dunwoody

ing. "Nothing is more satisfying than when you power up a project you've worked on for a week or a month and everything works great." She also likes the fact that she makes good money, takes long vacations (she gets five weeks a year), and has never, in her ten years in the business, had to look for a job.

Why Join the Union?

As a member of the St. Paul Local of the International Brotherhood of Electrical Workers, Julie lets the union do the looking for her. If she is laid off because a contractor doesn't have enough electrical work, her name goes on a list at the union hall, and when it comes to the top of the list she is called for work. If she gets sick and can't work, her insurance is still paid by the union. "It's very good health insurance," she says. "It would cost me $370 a month if I had to buy it myself." She also has two different pension plans and an annuity, all paid for by employers who want to work with union electricians and are willing to pay the money into the union benefit plans. "I could have chosen to work as a non-union electrician, but that's a whole different ballgame. With the union, you earn more money, you are better protected, you have better benefits, and you have some of the best training."

The union may find Julie a job working on any type of building. Her job title is "commercial-industrial inside wireman." (The language hasn't changed yet to reflect the fact that many women are entering the field.)

JULIE'S CAREER PATH

Gets accepted for apprenticeship with IBEW ▼

Becomes journeyman ▼

That means she is responsible for making sure the electrical wiring inside a building is installed properly aid, fire alarms, electrical transformers, and motor controls. "If I don't like working as a construction elec-

Unfortunately, there is a feeling that women don't belong in certain areas.

and works correctly and safely. "I feel proud when I hear people talking about some new building in town, and I say to myself 'I helped build that!'"

As a journeyman, Julie is eligible for free training from her union in many different areas of construction, including instrumentation, refrigeration, energy management, computer basics, programmable logic controllers, leadership training so she can lead a crew, safety and first trician or I want a change, I can choose to work as a maintenance electrician, or I can enter another area of the construction trade."

The First Years

Having a good paying job that challenges her both physically and mentally is important to Julie, who had to work three jobs at the same time to pay her bills before she became an electrician. But getting to journeyman status wasn't easy. In fact, the first years in the trade were pretty rough.

Julie worked during high school as well as after graduating. Before finding her profession as electrician, she worked in a plastics factory, running the presses; as a cook in a number of restaurants; stripping tobacco in Kentucky, where a friend had moved; in a bakery; at a metal factory; and for an electronics firm. None of the work paid her enough to have only one job.

Julie was working in Texas as a cook when the electrician who was dating her roommate asked her if she wanted to try electrical work. The man had his own small business and he needed a helper. Julie quit her three cooking jobs and went to work for him. But when he took off for a week without telling her and she had to answer complaints from customers, she decided it was time to leave that job and return to Minnesota, where she was born and raised.

Contractors in the construction trade in Texas had told Julie that Dunwoody

CAREER CHECKLIST ✓

You'll like this job if you ...

- Can take direction but also work independently
- Are strong enough to do the required tasks
- Love a challenge
- Can work with all types of people
- Are safety conscious

Technical Institute in Minneapolis was one of the best places in the country to get training as an electrician. So she headed for the twin cities of Minneapolis and St. Paul and entered Dunwoody. Unfortunately, about that time her sister died. Julie, who was doing drugs and alcohol, didn't make it through school. Two years later, she enrolled in St. Paul Technical Institute in the electrician's program. It was about this time that she quit drinking and taking drugs.

Julie was motivated to change her life. "From the time I was eleven, I was a sort of an addict. I was always non-traditional, and I just didn't know where I fit in, even though in sixth grade I had been the class president and head cheerleader. When I hit seventh grade, I thought I could have an identity as a bad girl."

The St. Paul program was rough for Julie. It was the mid 1980s, and there just weren't that many women in the trades yet. She had to contend with men who were threatened because she knew more than they did—having worked briefly as an electrician and having been in school for electrician work once. Students sabotaged her work and her class projects, and she endured lots of teasing because she was a woman. She had to wait to get into the union apprentice program for two years, during which time she supported herself with other jobs, such as

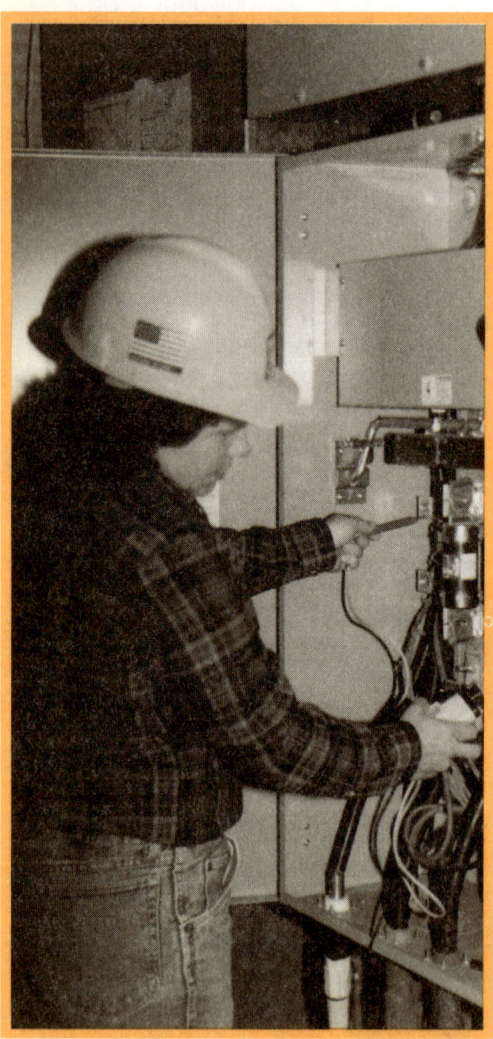

stripping the varnish from wood for a contractor remodeling old houses.

Once she got into the apprenticeship program, it was still difficult. The guys didn't believe she could do the work well, and she couldn't get the type of jobs she needed to get a well-rounded base of experience. But Julie was persistent. She stuck with it, continued to learn, kept her grades up (she had to go to night school two days a week for four years), and eventually began to get better work. It also helped that as time went on, more women entered the trade. "It used to be I was the only woman on the job. Now, there are always three or four women at the sites where I work. Even if I don't know them, or they don't like me, it makes a big difference just having other women there."

when things got tough. She traveled around the state to elementary schools to talk about her work, and to technical schools, talking to the women who were studying construction trades, telling them what she had learned about getting along on the job. She was partially responsible for publication of a reference guide with the different requirements for each union in Minnesota. "This was something that had really frustrated me. You couldn't even find out what the requirements were to get into the apprenticeship program. Today, they will tell you because they are desperate for workers."

These days, Julie enjoys kayaking, hiking, and being outdoors as much as possible. She thinks someday she will start her own business—something in the construction trade.

Support from Women's Groups

For many years, Julie was on the board of directors of her local Women in the Trades organization. She got support from this group of women

Margaret Nelson

Operating Engineer, Stewart Brothers, Atlanta, GA,
Member Operating Engineers Union, Local 926

Heavy Equipment Operator

She Shifts Gears to Build Highways

As a girl, Margaret Nelson loved to drive. "All the boys in my neighborhood could shift car gears by age 10, and I learned how, too. I got in trouble when I was young, driving our car without my Dad's permission."

Margaret finally got a chance to earn her living driving at age 45. "I was in Atlanta, coming home on the bus from my receptionist job, and I picked up this brochure about training women for jobs in the trades." It was 1996. Margaret took a day off from work and went to orientation to find out what was involved—12 weeks of training and then help getting a job.

"I always wanted to do this type of work. In the 1960s I had wanted to be a lineman for the telephone company,

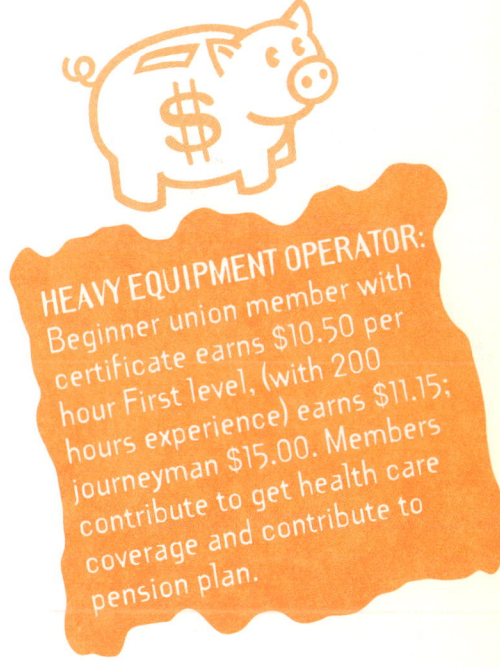

HEAVY EQUIPMENT OPERATOR: Beginner union member with certificate earns $10.50 per hour First level, (with 200 hours experience) earns $11.15; journeyman $15.00. Members contribute to get health care coverage and contribute to pension plan.

MARGARET'S CAREER PATH

- Graduates high school in Phoenix
- Marries, has 3 daughters
- Works receptionist jobs, attends college

but my folks said no. Then I wanted to join the service, but my folks said no. I thought 'I really want to do this!' I've equipment operator, because she would really need to earn money by the time training ended.

Because of the noise, we use hand signs—our own construction sign language.

taken chances before, bet on myself. If it didn't work out, I could always get someone to hire me as a receptionist."

So Margaret, who had been divorced since age 31, talked to her three grown daughters about her plans. With their support and her savings, she paid her bills, stocked her freezer with food, tightened her belt, and took the training. She focused on doing so well that she could immediately get a job as a heavy

"One of our speakers was a woman from an asphalt company. I asked her so many questions about the work using heavy equipment that she told me to come by her office at 6:00 a.m. to apply." Margaret showed up at 6:00 a.m. in her jeans, shirt, boots, hard hat, and her lunch, ready to work. After filling out the application, they sent her for a physical. "You had to take a drug test, but that's no problem for me. I told them to get the results

- Gets operator's certificate, can't get job
- Works as receptionist in college athletic department, takes classes
- Moves to Atlanta, takes training course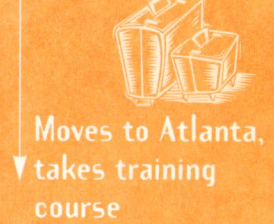

ASAP, which they did. I started work that same afternoon."

At last Margaret was a heavy equipment operator. She had a job with APAC McDougal-Warren working on building roads and parking lots. She immediately joined the Operating Engineers Union, Local 926. That was just the beginning.

A Chinese Backhoe

"My first day was absolutely horrible. The men didn't want to be bothered with me. Although there were five or six other women there, they were working in traffic or as labor, not as equipment operators. The foreman handed me a shovel. I said 'I'm an operator.' He said 'Well, operate this, you're a Chinese backhoe' (a backhoe machine is used to dig, and in the 1800s, Chinese laborers worked on the railroads, digging with shovels)." Even though she was doing a laborer's work, the company had to pay her operator's wages—a beginner earns

MARGARET'S CAREER PATH

▼ Gets job at asphalt company, joins union

▼ Gets enough hours to make top level operator

$10.50 per hour, with time and one half for overtime (more than 40 hours per week) and double time for Saturdays and Sundays.

"I worked 12-hour days, six days a week. I've got tenacity. I've been a single parent for years, which is more stressful. I hung in there." For one year, Margaret worked that shovel as a laborer, but every chance she got—when an equipment operator quit, got sick, or was fired—she operated the equipment. Operators had to have a certain amount of hours driving the equipment to reach higher pay levels. The foreman wouldn't turn in any time for Margaret, so she kept her personal calendar and wrote down each time she drove, even if it was only 15 minutes.

Though Margaret had trouble with foremen, and often was switched to other crews, the superintendents were watching her. They knew she worked hard and well, no matter what the foremen said. When Margaret had enough hours, she showed her calendar to the superintendent, and he gave her the hours on her record, which increased her pay. Then she took a stand and told her foreman she wasn't going to fill in any more. "I told him if he could not give me a job as operator, then leave me alone. I finally got the job."

From Dawn to Dusk

Margaret gets up at 5:00 a.m. to get ready for work. She packs her lunch and plenty of water. Sometimes she brings extra desserts or homecooking to share with members of her crew when they eat together. She wears bib overalls, a long-sleeved shirt (summer or winter), and work boots. She gathers her goggles, leather gloves, and hard hat. She drives her car, arriving at the yard by 6:15 a.m. Her equipment is loaded on trucks, if it isn't already on the job site, and she gets her hand tools. The first thing at the job site Margaret does is a routine maintenance check on her equipment, making sure oil and other fluids are okay, that things like fanbelts are tight, and everything is running properly. Then she warms up the machine and is ready to go by sun-up, picking up where she left off the day before. If it's a new job, she gets direction from the engineers at the site.

Margaret has learned how to build a road from the ground up—from pulling down a tree and cutting the path, to ordering the rocks, gravel, and asphalt. But now, where she works, that "rough" preparation is done by others. Margaret drives a front-end loader, a steel wheel packer, and a traffic roller. The loader picks up dirt and gravel and

CAREER CHECKLIST ✓

You'll like this job if you ...

- Like to work outdoors
- Are open minded and flexible
- Can work with all types of people
- Like to drive, will learn shifting
- Have a strong, determined personality
- Are tenacious, will never give up on what you want

moves it around. The packer runs over the dirt, then rock, then the aggregate (crushed smaller rock and gravel) to pack it down and make the road bed solid, firm, and smooth. After the asphalt is laid down, the traffic roller smoothes out any bubbles and prepares a smooth surface for the cars and trucks. If the temperature falls below 42 degrees, the asphalt gets too cold to roll out, so the crews do other types of work or go back to the yard to do equipment maintenance. There's a lot of noise driving these machines, so Margaret wears earplugs.

"It's my passion. I love seeing the finished product—that smooth surface. And I love getting that big paycheck."

Margaret admits this type of work is hard on families, especially with small children (her daughter and two grandchildren live with her). "Because you work so many hours, you have to build support systems—people who will drop off and pick up the children at day care. Saturdays are especially hard because my daughter works Saturdays too."

A Traditional Family

Margaret always felt nontraditional in a traditional family. "My brother and I would swap duties. I'd do the yard, and he'd do laundry. I loved being outside." Born on the Choctaw-Chickasaw Nations reservation (her mother is Native American, her father African/German American), Margaret moved to Phoenix with her family when she was four years old. "There were zero point one percent Blacks, in Phoenix at that time, but we were raised in a typical working class family. I, as the oldest daughter, had a lot of responsibility in the care of my brother and three sisters."

Margaret married right out of high school at age 17. For the next 20 years, she worked part-time jobs and cared for her three daughters. "When I got divorced, I decided to teach myself to be the best receptionist I could be, work part-time, and go to community college." When she was a part-time receptionist for a company that taught people how to operate heavy

equipment, Margaret got an opportunity to drive the big machines. She was so good at it that after just a few "lessons" they gave her a certificate. "It came easy to me, like driving a big car." But no one would hire her.

Margaret believes strongly in education. She decided to seek work at Arizona State University in nearby Tempe, Arizona, because as an employee she could get her classes free. "I tell my girls to keep taking classes. As long as you are in that atmosphere, you will work your way into what you want to do. College taught me how to communicate. Being educated, I felt I could talk to anybody about anything; no one could intimidate me."

Margaret enjoys being in the Atlanta area. "I have my church, which is my foundation. I have my home, a garden, and an ugly dog." When she's not cheering on the sporting teams of the Atlanta Braves or the Falcons, Margaret enjoys quilting and singing. She is also active with the women's training program at Goodwill Industries that got her started. She attends conferences, has been featured in publications, and spends time encouraging other women to join the trades.

Credit: Alan David Photography

Susan Byrd

Master Plumber, Plumber and Pipefitters Union, Local 72, Atlanta, GA
Major in Spanish

Master Plumber

Plumb Perfect!

Susan Byrd, who has been a plumber for 12 years, says it all started when she watched workers construct the Atlanta, Georgia, transportation network Marta. At the time, she was working in an office and thought construction work looked like fun. A friend knew a local plumber, Mitch Carey and Daughters. Susan contacted him.

"He hired me immediately. He knew I didn't know anything, but he was willing to teach me. I worked with him for seven months, and I liked it. He told me about the union, so I applied and was accepted."

Susan became an apprentice in the Plumbers and Pipefitters Union. "They put you to work immediately, because it's part of your training. You

PLUMBER: Apprentice $9 per hour, raises every six months if you pass your classes. Journeyman from $22.60 per hour Union members pay dues every month. Pension plan and vacation fund payments are deducted from weekly paycheck. You are eligible for health benefits providing you work a set amount of hours each quarter.

SUSAN'S CAREER PATH

Loves Spanish language   **Graduates Spelman College**    **Marries Jeffrey, has two sons**

also have to go to two-hour classes two nights a week, August through May." The apprenticeship is five years. The final step is to take the "turn out" test. "At the time I went, you had to rough out a bathroom, do an isometric drawing, then take the state test. Once you pass, you get your journeyman license and a higher wage."

All Kinds of Pipes

Susan works on all kinds of cast iron and copper pipes. It is her job to see that water goes where it is supposed to for use in water fountains, kitchens, hot water heaters, bathrooms, and any other uses. It's part of her job to see that waste water travels from those areas and goes where it is supposed to. She also prepares the air-vent pipes, so that toilets work properly and there are no sewage odors.

The big challenge is to do all this pipe work without any leaks. After the work is checked by a building inspector, Susan installs the fixtures—sinks, tubs, showers, and toilets. Susan usually works on large commercial buildings, like the Atlanta Olympic stadium or high-rise apartment buildings or office buildings, where there are many types of fixtures. Her most memorable jobs are Underground Atlanta, Atlanta Pretrial Detention Center, Marta, Phillips Arena, Georgia Dome, Hartsfield International Airport, and a Marriott Hotel.

Susan starts her day at 5:00 a.m. with a wake-up shower. She dresses in her work boots, jeans, and a T-shirt (the sleeves must be at least three

Works various jobs and substitute teaches  **Works with plumber as assistant**  **Joins union, starts apprenticeship**

inches long; in winter she wears long sleeved shirts or sweatshirts with a hood). Then she packs her breakfast and lunch, gathers her hard hat and gloves, and drives to work. By 6:30 a.m., she has to be at the work site "gang box," where everyone gathers and where they have safety meetings.

"Usually you work in teams, so my partner and I will gather our tools, which the company supplies. We each have our own basics—tape measure, level, and a pair of channel-lock pliers. Then, depending upon the work ahead, we'll gather tools like a drill and power cord, a portaband, tubing cutters to cut copper pipe, an acetylene tank for soldering, and a striker to light the torch."

Today, Susan is doing her favorite work. "I love running copper piping. I like the lines, the angles. I love to sit

back, when it's finished, and see what I've done. I really enjoy it when it tests out with no leaks."

Susan, who is 5 foot 3 inches and weighs 124 pounds, has to carry pipe, which comes in 10 foot lengths, and

SUSAN'S CAREER PATH

Becomes journeyman plumber

Becomes master plumber

other materials into the work area. For this job she is hanging the pipes from the ceiling, so Susan has to install a series of hangers that will hold the pipe up. She measures carefully, drills holes in the ceiling along the route the pipe will take, hammers anchors into the holes, uses a setting tool so the anchors won't come out, then cuts metal rods the proper length, attaches a hanger at the end of the rod (the pipe will rest in these hangers), and screws the rods into the anchors. Now she has a resting place for the pipe.

Next she cleans the copper pipe with a cleaning paste. She brings the pipe together by means of a coupling, heats it, and solders two pieces together, then hangs a section.

Susan follows drawings and prints that show where the pipes should go, and what sizes they should be. For example, a drawing may show to break off from the three-inch line to supply a one inch to a water heater, then supply an inch and one half pipe to the bathroom.

Susan's work day ends around 3:30. She does her errands on her way home.

Still a Man's World

Plumbing is an old, well-established trade, and the workers are mainly men. "I am either the only woman on the construction site, or there might be one woman electrician and one woman carpenter. The bathroom situation is horrendous, usually a portable jiffy john. The way I look at it, you're in a man's world, and the rough facilities go along with the territory." But if there are several women on the job, the women can request a separate john for the women.

"I've never had a problem with the guys, and I've always pulled my weight. You are constantly being taught how to do things the proper way, how to lift, how to read a drawing. You work with a partner, and some can get pretty protective of you. Even some of the men who feel women don't belong have changed their minds when they see a woman doing a good job and being serious about good work."

"I've seen some young girls get overwhelmed by all the guys flirting with them, this one and that one wanting to eat lunch with them. I think you can't do that; it sends the wrong message. I talk to everyone, but I'm there to work. Even though the business is male-oriented, one of my fondest experiences was having a female apprentice, Robin, to train under me. She is now a journeyman and doing quite well teaching plumbing at Job Corps in California."

CAREER CHECKLIST ✓

You'll like this job if you ...

- Not afraid of hard work
- Like to learn by doing
- Like to work with your hands
- Don't mind having another check your work
- Have a sense of humor
- Can get along with all kinds of people, especially men
- Can stay focused on what you want

Not a Tomboy

Susan grew up in Brooklyn, New York in the Williamsburg projects. "They were nice back then. I did lots of things like ice skating at Rockefeller Center, going to museums and the theater. I had lots of friends, boys and girls. I wasn't a tomboy, but I've always been comfortable with males. I have four brothers, two older and two younger. A lot of my friends are males, and I seem to relate better to males."

Susan liked music and loved to read. In fifth grade she started taking languages and found she really loved Spanish. She was good in track, but never pursued it. Because she and her cousin were close, and because she and her parents didn't like the high schools in Brooklyn, she went to Fayetteville, North Carolina, lived with her grandmother, and attended the E.E. Smith High School with her cousin (the same high school her mother attended). After graduation, she

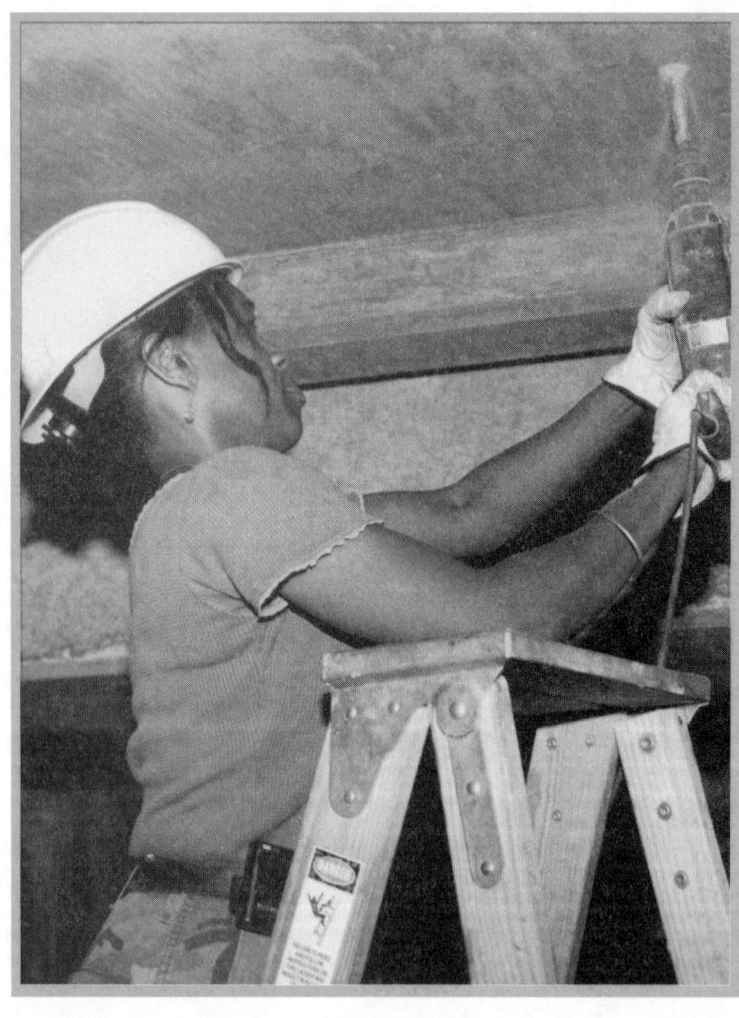

went to Spelman College in Atlanta. She majored in Spanish, thinking she'd get an interpreter's job, maybe with an airline. She took a minor in education because if she taught a certain number of years, she wouldn't have to pay back her student loan. But after experiencing her student teaching, she decided she didn't want to spend all her days in school, so she never got a certificate to teach.

While at college, Susan met Jeffrey, and they've been together ever since—they just celebrated their 20th anniversary. The next few years, Susan worked various jobs—doing the news at radio station WCLK in Atlanta, deejay at a club, cocktail waitress—and had two sons. She also steadily did substitute teaching. (You didn't have to have a certificate, just a degree.)

A Master Plumber

When Susan started her plumbing apprenticeship, the family's life changed. "I couldn't have done it without Jeffrey's support. During the day, the boys would be in school and we'd both be at work. But on the nights I had classes, Jeffrey would take on the responsibilities of the house. Now he works in food and beverages."

Susan recently passed the exam and is now a master plumber. That means she is licensed to run her own business. She is planning her future. "I want to work for the union. I'll be a contractor and start small. I'd like to work on schools. There's really no limit."

> The way I look at it, you're in a man's world. The rough facilities go along with the territory.

Hilary Colbert

Electrician Apprentice, Electrical Construction Co., Portland, OR
Member, International Brotherhood of Electrical Workers

Electrician, Apprentice

All the Right Connections

Four years ago, Hilary Colbert made a tough decision—to become an apprentice electrician. She was working two jobs to support herself and her 11-year-old daughter. She would lose $600 a month in income, but if she could do the work, the promise was higher wages in the years ahead.

"I had heard about the apprenticeship from my high school basketball coach, who told me one of my classmates had entered the program, enjoyed it, and was working on a regular basis. I have always been fascinated by electricity and curious about it. I thought, all I can do is try and see whether or not it will work out for me. I told my daughter 'we'll pinch here and there, and in the long run we'll be 110 percent better off.'"

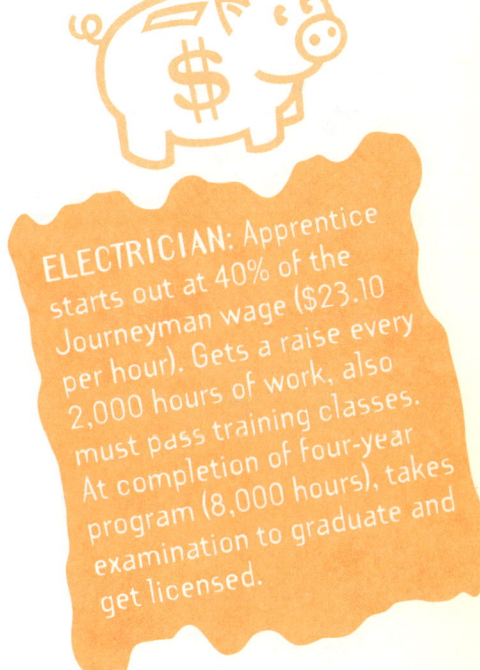

ELECTRICIAN: Apprentice starts out at 40% of the Journeyman wage ($23.10 per hour). Gets a raise every 2,000 hours of work, also must pass training classes. At completion of four-year program (8,000 hours), takes examination to graduate and get licensed.

HILARY'S CAREER PATH

- Loves sports, plays on high school basketball team
- Has daughter, attends college
- Works several jobs, cares for ill mother

Today, Hilary is better off. She makes $8 more per hour, has great benefits, enjoys the work, and she looks forward to becoming a journeyman electrician and earning more than $23 per hour.

What Type of Electrician?

At the IBEW union, there were 90 openings for the 5-year apprentice program when Hilary and 700 other people applied. "To qualify, I had to have Algebra I and II, be 18 years old, and have a valid driver's license. Then I had an intense interview before the board of eight people. It was tough, but I did get called back for the second interview. However, I didn't make the cut."

Hilary was disappointed that she didn't get accepted as a commercial electrician apprentice. But she was told there were two other programs

Adds evening job as school security ▼

Gets full-time job at boot manufacturer ▼

Hires on as apprentice, limited energy program ▼

she qualified for—residential and limited energy. She thought about it overnight, then checked to make sure her enrollment would not make her ineligible for future opportunities in the commercial program (which paid more). The union said she was still elgible. So she decided to enter the limited energy program.

Hilary gave notice at her full-time job with a boot manufacturer and registered for the training. Two weeks later she started and was immediately dispatched by the union to work for Christianson Electric.

"The job was at a bank in town. I joined a group of five men. They took me by the hand and helped me learn about the tools and the terminology. I didn't know anything. They told me what was expected of me. I started by pulling and labeling cable."

Hilary appreciates the help she got. "They took time and effort above and beyond the call of duty. In a close-knit industry like this, not all guys are as open to you as a newcomer, never mind being female. I let them know what they did for me is truly appreciated. It makes me want to help other newcomers. Some guys think 'she's here to take my job.' But I'm not, I'm there to make a job for myself and a better industry for everyone."

After a few months, an opening came up in the commercial apprenticeship program. "I thought about changing, but I was very happy where I was. Also, I'd be working outside a lot. I'd rather be indoors, so I decided not to switch. I've been extremely happy."

HILARY'S CAREER PATH

- Works on voice and data equipment
- Works in hospital setting

Her Work Helps People

In the limited energy field, Hilary works with low voltage electricity, which is used by voice and data communication. She works on telephones, computers, fire alarms, communication systems, and hooking up various electronic products. In her training classes she studies Ohms law (the strength of a direct current is directly proportional to the potential difference and inversely proportional to the resistance of the circuit), electricity theory, local area networks, fibre optics, and the history of NECA (the National Electrical Code) and code books, because installations must be made according to regulations and pass inspection.

As a four-year apprentice, Hilary still often works with a journeyman, but she has enough hours to work alone sometimes. Hilary works by herself at her current job at a hospital where she installs communication devices.

"What I love about the work is the contact with people. Here in the hospital environment, I'm helping fill many needs. It's a good feeling."

Hilary arrives on the job early and gets the work orders for the day or finishes up what she was working on the previous day. "For example, most of the communication equipment is in a closet—phone switches, hubs for computers, and the cables. To install a telephone line, say for a computer, I pull cable from the closet to the station or desk. Then I cut in a box, place it (usually on the floor), and install the phone jack, maybe a multiple line. I test it, do the paperwork, and get the customer to sign off that it is working properly."

Hilary also installs the nurse-call equipment, so patients can push a button and a light comes on at the nurses desk showing which room needs attention. "For nurse call cabling, I have to be sure all lines are tied in and working properly." Hilary also does problem solving. "When trouble shooting, you don't always know the answer. You have to decide whether to call a coworker, your journeyman or the customer, or contact the product manufacturer."

Sometimes Hilary takes a job out of town. Then, in addition to her hourly wage, she is paid a per diem—a set amount of money to cover her food and lodging. She has a good friend in her neighborhood who cares for her daughter when she has to be out of town.

Love of Family

Hilary grew up in Massachusetts. She moved to Portland, Oregon, with her mother and three sisters, when she was 10. In middle school she played several sports, and in high

CAREER CHECKLIST

You'll like this job if you ...

- Like to work with your hands
- Have a curiosity about electricity, want to learn about it
- Have a respect for electricity, will learn safe practices
- Have a positive attitude
- Are willing to do hard work and will make an extra effort
- Like to work indoors

GROUNDBREAKERS

International Support Network

In 1953, a group of 16 women who were working in the construction industry got together to provide a support network for each other. They called it Women in Construction of Fort Worth (Texas). Two years later, it became the National Association of Women in Construction. In recent years, NAWIC affiliated with NAWIC-Australia and NAWIC New Zealand.

With approximately 6,200 members in 200 chapters in 47 states and 3 Canadian provinces, NAWIC's mission is to promote and support the advancement and employment of women in the construction industry. It does this through its Foundation that offers programs for students from grade school to high school, introducing them to careers in construction. The Foundation offers accredited programs through Clemson University. The Foundation and AWICA chapters award scholarships to college students pursuing construction-related studies.

school she was on the basketball team. She went to Mt. Hood College to major in business management, hoping to own a business some day. Then her mother got ill. Hilary, at age 21, dropped out of college to get work to help support herself, her daughter, her mother, and to help with the medical bills. Her older sister and the younger twins were just getting into universities at the time.

"I've been working two or three jobs at a time since then." Hilary worked at a restaurant at first and later got a full-time job with a boot manufacturer. Then she got a second job as a campus security guard at a night school, where she works 5:30 to 9:30 p.m., Monday through Thursday. "For the past nine years I've had that job. I enjoy it. The kids are really good, and they want to be there. The night school is held in part of my old high school, so I feel I'm giving something back. I work from September through June. Because of my apprenticeship classes, which are two nights a week, someone else works in my place those two nights."

In the summertime, Hilary works part-time for a Greek restaurant.

When Hilary's mother died, Hilary's sisters were out of college and on their own. Financially, things were better. "I decided it was time for me." That's when she entered the apprenticeship program, quit her full-time job, and only kept one part-time job.

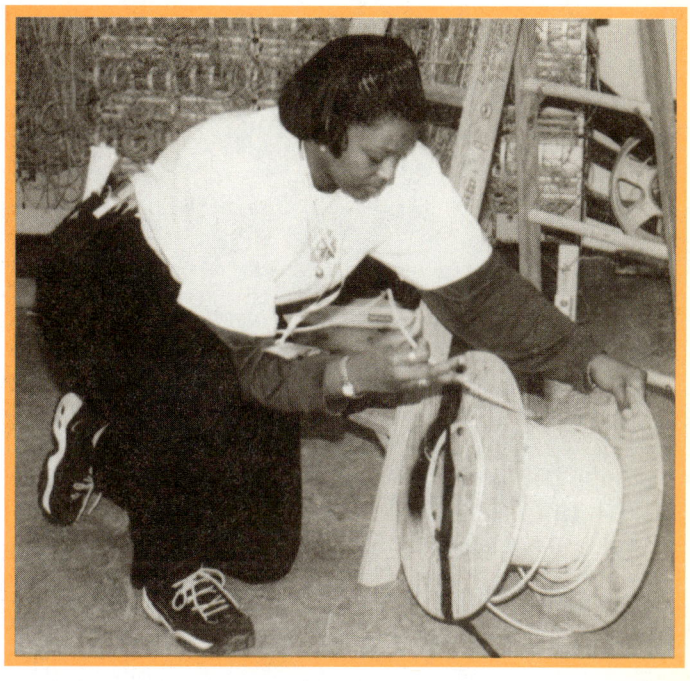

Because Hilary works so many hours, her free time is limited. She spends most of it with family. "We're very close. We have family get-togethers, celebrate birthdays and holidays." Recently, Hilary joined the Oregon Trade Women's Network. "We have monthly meetings and I've volunteered to go out to the schools and explain about my work. We take a light bulb and give a demonstration how it works, then explain switches, and put the whole puzzle together. We encourage the kids to get their math skills and if they think they're interested, to take a basic electric or electronic course."

One of Hilary's union benefits is a vacation fund that her employer contributes to, according to the hours she works each week. The money goes into a credit union account and Hilary can use it for vacation, emergencies, or anything she wants. Maybe she'll use it for a vacation celebration when she completes her apprenticeship and becomes a journeyman electrician.

Kristin Gunderson

Staff Carpenter, St. Paul Ramsey/Regions Hospital, St. Paul, MN
Major in Education

Carpenter, Journeyman

Crafting a Career She Loves

When Kristin A. Gunderson goes to work at St. Paul Ramsey Hospital she drives her '95, GMC, extended-cab truck. Kris is a staff carpenter, and she will use the truck to carry tools and materials when she works at sites away from the main building. Kris works from 7:30 a.m. until 4:00 p.m., five days a week.

"Each morning I check the work orders to see what needs to be done", says Kris. "It may be fixing a door that is hard to shut by putting on new hinges or planing it, replacing ceiling tiles because of water damage, or attaching shelving. I schedule my own work, but I have to contact the person needing the work and arrange when I can do it. It takes some negotiating because in the hospital I have to work

CARPENTER: Staff carpenter at hospital: the hospital pays union scale wage, $24 per hour for journeyman. The hospital contributes into health benefits and pension plans for employees.

UNION CARPENTER: Regular contractor employer pays union scale wage, $24 per hour for journeyman worker. Apprentice starts at $12 and gets increase every 1,000 hours worked. Overtime pays time and one-half (for example, $12 plus $6 = $18 per hour). Employee contributes to health plan and pension plan set up by the union.

KRISTIN'S CAREER PATH

▼ Works on family farm, loves sports  ▼ Graduates college  ▼ Teaches phys. ed., coaches

around nurses, doctors, and others. For example, I can not be making noise drilling or hammering near the operating section when they are doing surgery."

Kris is a journeyman carpenter and union member and works in the facilities services department with other trades people. The three carpenters have carts with drawers and cabinets so they can carry their tools and the materials they use—like nails, screws, and doorknobs. They don't wear uniforms, but must look clean and neat. Kris wears jeans, a buttoned shirt (no T-shirts), and regulation work boots.

"I love this work. You create your stuff, and if it doesn't quite work, you can change it. You are able to satisfy someone. Someone wants something done, and they need that from you, and you can provide it. It is very rewarding."

When Kris first started at the hos-

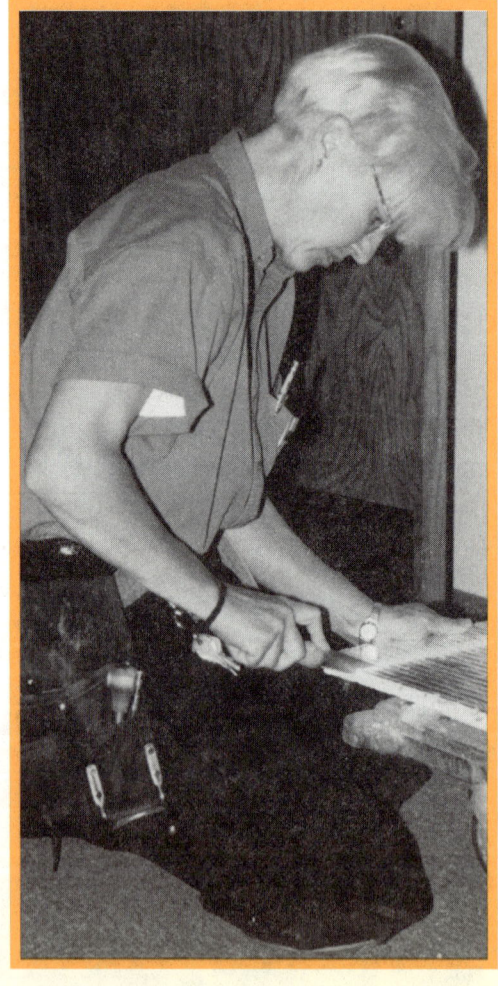

Becomes apprentice, moves to Minneapolis   **Works weather-proofing homes**    **Works residential, new and remodeling**

pital in 1989, most of the work was carpentry unique to hospitals—building special cabinets or shaping countertops to fit a special space. Now the work is more maintenance and repair. "I still find it challenging because I'm always learning. I have learned how to work clean, without a lot of mess. I've learned how the hospital is constructed—for example, gas lines are in some of the walls, which limits how you attach things."

A Farmer's Daughter

Kris grew up in rural Wisconsin on her parents' dairy farm in Poynette. "I was a highly active kid, the 'end' of six children. I worked a lot around the farm with my father and two brothers, so I had a pretty good understanding of working with men."

Kris didn't think about what she wanted to do until high school. She was successful at athletics—track and field, high jump, softball—and decided to become a physical education teacher. She graduated from the University of Wisconsin-Stevens Point with a degree in Education. After a year coaching basketball at Bayport High School and working in a nearby canning factory, Kris got a teaching job at Ellsworth Junior High in Ellsworth.

"I taught in junior high, then senior high, but at the end of two years I grew restless telling kids what to do. I wanted to do something hands on."

To make her decision, Kris made a list of things she wanted in her work day. "I wanted more physical activity—to be on my feet, work with my hands. I wanted a 40-hour week with

KRISTIN'S CAREER PATH

▼ Works commercial jobs

▼ Gets job at Regina Hospital

no weekend work. I was coaching weekends and teaching during the week. Back in 1981, I was making only $11,500 and that was low pay."

As Kris investigated different types of work, she spoke with local carpenters. "One was my friend's brother. He'd talk about his workday and it appealed to me. So that summer I went to visit friends in the city, St. Paul, and looked in the phone directory's white pages for the carpenter's union."

Kris called the union and asked how she could become a carpenter. The answer—she had to find a union contractor to take her on as an apprentice, to work alongside an experienced carpenter and learn. Since Kris still lived in Wisconsin, she found it hard to find a union contractor in St. Paul. She asked the union business agent if he would contact her if anything came up, and she went back home. She had signed up to teach that next fall, but about midsummer, the union called her. She went for an interview and got a job at Natural Resources Corporation in Minneapolis. She quit her teaching job and became a union apprentice.

From Apprentice to Journeyman

"The union pay was $6.81 per hour, which was lower than my teacher's pay. But after every 1,000 hours of work you got an increase. This was high incentive to me. I was eager to work, and I knew I'd get a raise, so the pay would build up quickly—much faster than my teacher's salary would increase."

Every two weeks, apprentices had to spend an 8-hour day at the union school in formal training, things like framing and how to use a plane. "We had to buy the basic tools—hammer, pliers, handsaw, and a combination square—which cost me about $50. As you went along, you followed the checklist of tools to purchase; so by the time you were a third year apprentice you had a pretty good group of tools. If you didn't have the right tools, you couldn't learn to do the work." After 244 hours of classroom work and 7,000 hours on the job, an apprentice could become a certified journeyman and earn a higher wage. (That's about three and one-half or four years, similar to time spent in college.)

Kris started out working in a crew of three—a journeyman carpenter and two apprentices. She learned how to weatherize homes to keep heating costs down. She did weather stripping, insulation and caulking, and replaced doors and windows. The non-profit company's mission was not only to help low-income people improve their housing, but also to hire women

CAREER CHECKLIST

You'll like this job if you …

- Like to work with your hands
- Like to create things
- Like to tear things apart, beat on things (rough carpentry)
- Are precise, like to make things attractive (finish carpentry)
- Have lots of energy
- Like to be doing things or you get bored
- Have good self-esteem

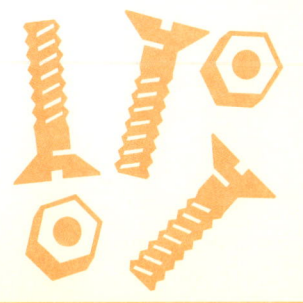

and minorities as apprentices and give them lots of training so they could do the work.

"I loved it. I learned how to do things with my hands. It was being creative with tools. You use your brain and it is physical—a great combination. The work was steady and I learned quickly. I am eager to constantly do things, so I was productive, which the company appreciated."

After about a year, Kris thought she needed new skills to keep herself marketable, able to get different jobs. She drove by some townhouses under construction and stopped to talk to the supervisor about working on them. She left her name and that evening got a call to come to work. "People do move around in the construction field, so it was not unusual for me to quit on short notice and move to another contractor. Also, since I was making more money, Natural Resources was glad to replace me with a lower paid apprentice and happy to see me doing well and moving up."

Kris got a variety of experience in residential work, building new homes and remodeling older homes. But residential construction was gradually being taken over by non-union

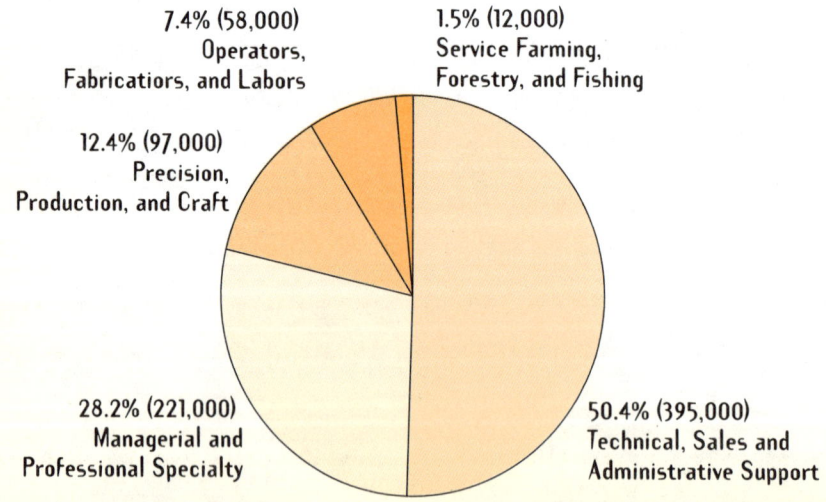

Jobs Held by Women in Construction (total: 784,000)

- 7.4% (58,000) Operators, Fabricatiors, and Labors
- 1.5% (12,000) Service Farming, Forestry, and Fishing
- 12.4% (97,000) Precision, Production, and Craft
- 28.2% (221,000) Managerial and Professional Specialty
- 50.4% (395,000) Technical, Sales and Administrative Support

Source: Bureau of Labor Statistics—Current Population Survey

contractors. Kris felt that to stay marketable as a union carpenter and to get higher wages, she would need commercial experience. She quit and went to work for a commercial contractor. Her first job was in south Minneapolis setting up concrete forms (which means building frames of wood) and monitoring the concrete pourers. "I also got to be a good caulker. I got to do a lot of finish caulking, giving a nice smooth finish to the caulking exposed to view."

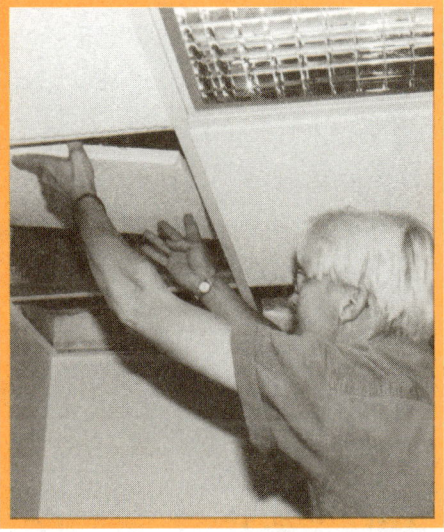

In July 1985, Kris got her journeyman certificate. Her next job was as lead carpenter overseeing apprentices for the Urban Coalition Weatherization Company. The owner of Urban Coalition had met Kris when she started out at Natural Resources. "When we had a new product or application to help weatherize the homes, we would go over to Urban and do team teaching. The head of the company, who really was interested in empowering women, remembered me, had found where I was working, and asked me to join his company as lead carpenter."

But in a few months, Natural Resources had an opening for a lead carpenter and offered the job to Kris, plus more money and her own van, so she didn't have to use her truck. She worked there three years before getting restless again.

"I left to take a commercial job. We built a parking ramp. We had to build large wall forms for concrete, so it involved heavy loads and hard physical labor. I'm not a large person, and it got old fast. I called the local union business agent and said, 'You've got to find me something good.' I'd kept a good relationship with him, and he got me in contact with Regions Hospital. I've been here 10 years now, and I love it."

Working with Men

Kris is the only trades woman in the hospital's facilities services. The other two carpenters and the electricians, plumbers, and painters are men. During her career, she has done well working with men. But Kris says that, although it is getting better, there is still a broad, sometimes subtle, disapproval of women working in the trades.

there are the men who like to get under your skin, who do things to irritate you. For those men I just don't respond. I look at them like 'you're wasting your energy.' Then there are the men who won't say anything to your face, but will tell your partner (the person you're working with) bad things about you. But your partner and the people who know you know the truth. You can't let it bother you."

Kris says that at first she'd get angry; she was frustrated because

> It is very rewarding. But there are the men who like to get under your skin, who do things to irritate you. For those men, I just don't respond.

"I've been called every name you can imagine, but not to my face. I manage to find the loyalists, men who have good relationships with their wives and daughters. If you do the work and you mind your own business, most men will work well with you. But she was trying to learn and be good at what she was doing. "I felt they weren't even giving me a chance. But I learned very quickly that if I did not give that anger and frustration any energy, it would not manifest itself."

Kris belongs to a group called Women in the Trades. The women get together socially once a month to talk about issues on the job and support each other. "You have to have your own self-esteem and self-motivation, because the people on the job aren't there to build your self-confidence."

When Kris isn't on the job, she likes to spend her time hiking and camping. She enjoys walking her friend's dogs in a nearby wooded city park. She likes to read, go to the theater, and on vacations she likes to see the museums and visit grand hotels with their carved fireplaces and woodwork. Kris recently bought a small home in St. Paul which she is fixing up. She plans to sell it in the spring and will probably buy another "fixer upper."

Kris plans on getting a master's degree in business, going to school nights and weekends. She hopes eventually to work as a manager of a large contractor company or become a contractor herself. "As women and minorities become more of the workforce, we will need to be in positions of power. I want to be ready. Women are

very suited to this trade, and women are needed, because we're good at communication and networking, which is important to being successful."

Credit: Kight Photography

Glenda Kelly

Apprentice, Sheetmetal Workers Union, Local 16, Portland, OR

Sheetmetal Worker, Apprentice

She Knows How the Air Flows

Overnight, 24-year-old Glenda Kelly changed from being an office worker to being a sheetmetal worker. She had never really considered doing this type of work, but one evening as she listened to her brother persuade her boyfriend to consider joining the Sheetmetal Workers Union, she was impressed. "My brother was talking about the excellent benefits, the retirement plan, the wages. Then, as he described the work and training on the job, I thought, 'I could do that.'"

Glenda and her boyfriend called the Local 16 in Portland, Oregon, and attended the next orientation. They filled out applications and put their names on the job list as pre-apprentices. "I

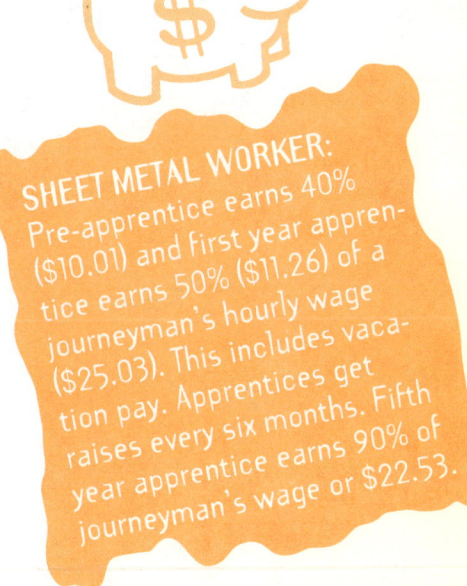

SHEET METAL WORKER: Pre-apprentice earns 40% ($10.01) and first year apprentice earns 50% ($11.26) of a journeyman's hourly wage ($25.03). This includes vacation pay. Apprentices get raises every six months. Fifth year apprentice earns 90% of journeyman's wage or $22.53.

GLENDA'S CAREER PATH

Likes softball, dances

Graduates high school

Does office work, has daughter

didn't quit my office job, but I signed up for a geometry course at the community college because I needed that to qualify for the apprentice program."

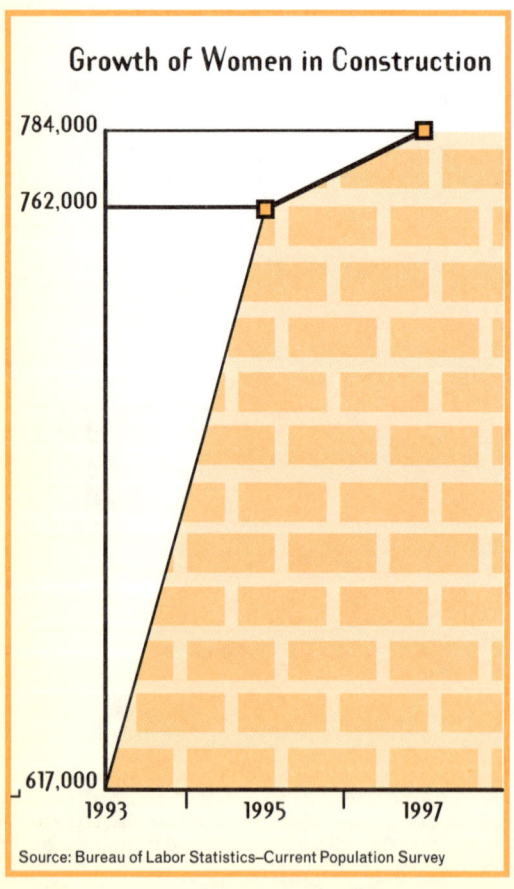

Growth of Women in Construction
784,000 — 1997
762,000 — 1995
617,000 — 1993
Source: Bureau of Labor Statistics–Current Population Survey

A Great Group of Guys

Soon Glenda got a phone call from a contractor to come to work at 7:00 a.m. the next day. "That was a Tuesday. I filled out paperwork and they gave me general information. Wednesday I was on the job as a pre-apprentice sheetmetal worker."

When Glenda arrived on the job site, she felt a little intimidated and scared. "I didn't know anyone, didn't know what to expect. But I was lucky to work with a great group of guys. They sat me down and explained everything to me—the hardware, the different tools we were using. I had no clue, so they explained what they needed from me."

The crew of about 60 workers was installing duct work in a new area

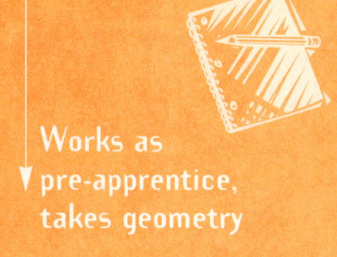

- Applies at Sheetmetal Workers Union
- Works as pre-apprentice, takes geometry
- Asks company to sponsor her apprenticeship

called a clean room—an area that had to be sterile, free of any germs and contamination. The installers would call for pieces of ductwork or tools on their radios. Then Glenda and the other workers would wipe down the ductwork to clean it and pass it through to the installers. The next day, Glenda "suited up" in the sterile garment and helped inside the room.

"I enjoyed it. The guys were like a bunch of big brothers, and I felt comfortable around them. Growing up, I was a tomboy and hung out with the guys. But I was sort of shocked, because I thought I'd get a hard time

In a new building, you're out there with no windows or doors, just a big open slab out in the weather.

about 'a woman doing a man's job.' I never got that. There were a few other women sheetmetal workers on the crew and women in the other trades like pipefitter and carpenter. But I think I got the best bunch of guys in all the trades." Glenda's journeyman was a couple of years younger than she was, but several men were around her age.

GLENDA'S CAREER PATH

Starts apprentice classes

Works on sustaining crew

Sponsored as an Apprentice

Glenda earned her geometry credit and the required three months of work hours, but there were no openings in the apprentice program. Then she learned that if she had 2,000 hours, the union would take her as an apprentice if a company sponsored her. "I was still working for the same company, so when I got 2,000 hours, I asked if they would sponsor me. They said I was doing a good job and agreed to sponsor me."

As an apprentice, Glenda now could start attending the training classes for the five-year program. She takes time off the job (gets state unemployment pay) to attend a week of concentrated training about every two months throughout the year. Then she returns to the same job. She has had classes in math—learning how to measure and figure dimensions and

distances— for example, to hang ductwork from the ceiling. She also has taken shop classes. Glenda's work experience has been in installation, but sheetmetal workers also need to know the shop work—fabrication, how to build duct work according to plan specifications, the different insulations, and the different types of pipe. These pipes carry airflow—hot air, cold air, and some air exhausts full of chemicals.

"The inside of some pipes are Teflon coated, like pots and pans, so corrosive elements won't eat through and leak. There are square duct pipes and stainless steel round pipe that goes from 4 inch to 72 inches in diameter. For general exhaust there is galvanized pipe, and there is also an OC pipe (other chemicals) because even though the exhaust is just air, it leaves deposits that can seep out."

Build, Demolish, and Maintain

Work starts at 6 a.m. The first thing the workers do are flex and stretch

CAREER CHECKLIST

You'll like this job if you ...

Get along with all kinds of people

Will do what you're told, don't always have to do it your way

Will work hard and learn quickly

Can take a joke

Are willing to take constructive criticism

Will study math to figure distances and dimensions

GROUNDBREAKERS

Journeyman Plasterer Instructor at Job Corps

Maybelle "May" Hartness is a student turned instructor of the U.S. Job Corps Training Program. In 1992, she became the first female plasterer hired as an instructor in the 30-year history of the program.

May enrolled in the Plasterers Program after quitting school at age 15. She excelled in her work and became the first female to compete in the International Apprenticeship Competition, where she placed in the top 10. She later served as the first female judge at the 1991 California State Apprenticeship Competition.

May has the task of teaching economically and emotionally disadvantaged young people the basic of the plastering trade. Her students not only stayed enrolled in the program but also have high placement records. She teaches young women how they, too, can be accomplished in a male-dominated industry, which many times be the most difficult aspect of work in construction. Young men also see May as a role model as she shows them how to accept women on the job.

Source: National Association of Women in Construction, Fort Worth, TX

exercises. Then it is time for "tool box talk." The foreman comes out and explains the work for the day, answers any questions, solves problems, and discusses any safety issues, safety memos, or new training.

Glenda's job on the construction site was to learn as quickly as possible and to do what she was told. "I really didn't know anything, so I appreciated the guys explaining to me what to do. Often they would stop me and say, 'look, try it this way, it's easier.'" Safety is an important aspect of construction work, especially in areas where many workers are doing different jobs. Glenda wears a hard hat, safety goggles, and work boots. When there are forklifts on the floor, she has to wear an orange safety vest so she'll be seen easily.

The materials on the site are fabricated in the shop, but they may not be quite the correct length. So Glenda has learned how to handle the saws, to cut the various pipes, and to assemble the hardware used to attach pipe to ceiling and walls.

After the new building work is completed, Glenda does a variety of fix-it work. "We solve any problems with the new pipe, if it wasn't properly installed or some worker damaged it by accident. There are gauges on the pipes that monitor for leaks, so we know when there is a problem. We find the leaks (often where the pipes are bolted together) and patch them, usually by tightening the bolts and gaskets that seal the connection between pieces of pipe."

Glenda also has worked in old buildings where she has done demolition work, tearing out old pipes and installing new ones. She is now a member of what is called a sustaining crew. "There are eight of us, and it's our job to make any changes that are needed, to do new jobs, and to fix leaks. If something is wrong, we find it and fix it. I enjoy it."

Born and raised in Portland, Glenda has a lot of family support in caring for her daughter, Kelsey, who is four years old. "Gramma and Grampa take her in the mornings and see that she gets to the Learning Center. It's a combination of school and child care. Since I get off work about 2:30 p.m., I can pick her up around 3." Kelsey thinks mom's job is great. "She has her dolls and toy kitchen, but she also has her own little tool belt and hard hat that she plays with. She knows that she can do whatever she wants to do when she grows up, just like her mom."

Tonia Burnette

Senior Associate, Tobey + Davis, Reston, VA
Major in Architecture

Architect

She Plans Beautiful and Useful Buildings

In the sixth grade, Tonia Burnette read that the best mixture of art and mathematics can be found in architecture. A painter from the age of 6 and also a whiz at math, Tonia decided at 11 that she wanted to be an architect. She followed her dream through high school drafting classes and then architectural school and into a job designing buildings. Today Tonia, now 39, designs hospitals and other healthcare buildings. She is a senior associate at the architecture firm Tobey + Davis in Reston, Virginia.

Tonia usually works 15 to 25 projects at the same time. She will juggle the work of three or four major clients each year. Usually her clients will ask her to work on several pro-

ARCHITECT: Starting salary low to mid $30,000s. After five years, $40,000 plus. Partners/associates make up to $200,000 per year.

TONIA'S CAREER PATH

Paints and has an art show  Takes drafting classes, builds model of school and The Louvre Graduates from college

jects. For example, Tonia is working with the University of Virginia Health Sciences Center to create a master plan for outpatient clinics. The master plan will show which currently existing outpatient clinics can be combined with other existing clinics for greater efficiency and also where new clinics need to be built for patient convenience or to compete with other hospitals. At the same time, Tonia is working various other projects with the Health Sciences Center—to build a pediatric outpatient center, to convert an old tub room to an office, and to build a new student clinic.

For another hospital, Tonia is creating a master plan that will incorporate the hospital's strategic goals: to increase the number of senior citizens and women who use the hospital and to increase the efficiency of the emergency room and of insurance claims processing. While none of these goals is

- Only woman architect at HDR
- Lands job at small firm in Washington, DC
- Oversees Job Corps facility buildings

directly connected to building the new facilities, they all result in building-related issues that Tonia and her team of architects must understand to design the best building. Tonia works with hospital personnel to answer questions such as: How accessible is the hospital for senior citizens, and how can it be made more accessible? Where should patients enter the emergency room? What should the design for equipment in the ER look like? Where should the claims processing department be located?

A Consultant To Clients

To get enough information to make good decisions about how hospital facilities ought to be built, Tonia will interview managers in different hospital departments. Sometimes she will interview as many as 200 people before a design is created. "We want to solve the big problems, but also all the little problems that drive people crazy. What I always say about architecture is that you have to go in with a microscope and come out with the big picture. If you don't look at the detail, you are going to miss the building blocks that are used to create the final building, and if you don't look at the big picture, you will have all these building blocks that don't result in a whole that is both beautiful and useful."

Creating and building master plans are long-term projects; they can take as much as seven years to complete. "You become very good friends with the people at the hospital and they count on you to understand what they need over the long-term."

87

TONIA'S CAREER PATH

Joins ▼ Tobey + Davis Architects  Becomes Associate, ▼ then Senior Associate of the firm

The Stages of Architecture

Generally, a health care building project will go through six stages. The first step is programming. After Tonia and her team have gathered enough information, they will put together a number of design alternatives with different price tags. The hospital staff will go over these suggestions and will pick the one that solves the most problems, after determining how much money they can afford to spend. Once a budget has been established, a site for the new building will be chosen. Then the architects move to the second stage—planning. At this stage, some of the details of the building's design begin to be filled in. For example, a building determined to be 40,000 square feet in stage one could be from one to three stories. At the planning stage, the number of stories is determined and what will be on each floor is decided.

The next stage is schematic design, where the architect starts roughing out the actual space. Rooms are drawn and the general look of the building is finalized. What will the elevation (outside) look like? Where does the equipment go and how will it be hidden from view? What sort of building material will be used? At the planning stage, engineering consultants are called in to answer questions about how the internal systems of the building, such as plumbing and heating and air conditioning, will be incorporated.

At the fourth stage, called design development, more details of the design are decided. The architects continue to work with the engineers to finalize the internal building systems. Materials get selected—the architect may have had brick in mind all the time, but at this stage the color and type of brick are decided. Or maybe the architect wants stone as the building material. The type of stone is chosen. Specifications for the type of roof, the way the walls will be built, and all the materials that will be needed to complete the building are made. A list of all things that will be a part of the building is prepared. Construction drawings of the various areas are made. Construction documents that specify exactly how things are to be built—the type of materials to be used and the way the materials should be placed—are created. Officials from the city, county, state, and federal government review the plans to make sure they conform to existing building codes--laws about how and where hospitals can be built.

The fifth stage is bidding and negotiation. Generally a number of building contractors will use the construction documents to submit

CAREER CHECKLIST ✓

You'll like this job if you ...

- Have a lot of initiative
- Have a high energy level to work long hours
- Can work well on a team
- Enjoy solving problems, the more problems the better
- Can stand up to anybody if you need to
- Are good at math and art

bids on what it would cost to build the hospital or clinic. The architect helps the hospital decide who gets the contract, based on company capability and price. The architect is always involved in some way during the building process to make sure the owners are getting what is specified in the construction documents.

Tonia is most heavily involved with projects during the early stages of the design process. Architects who work with her may do the actual design, once all the determinations for what is needed are made and ways to solve the problems presented are decided. Tonia also may be heavily involved at the end of the process, as the project is built. She will visit the site to make sure the contractors use the materials specified and build according to the documents.

"We have to make sure the contractor is giving the owners what they paid for. This process can be somewhat adversarial. In the best cases, everybody works together and if there is a problem we just work together to solve it. But sometimes the contractors are just looking for ways to make more money, and then you have to be really tough. This is where being a woman can sometimes be difficult. The main thing is, you have to try to stay calm At the construction site, you cannot show any weakness. Strength wins. Sometimes I get called in to be

the 'heavy hitter,' or 'the bulldog.' Even though it's the least favorite part of what I do, I have learned to do it well. It's just part of the job."

She Helps Run the Office

Because Tonia is a senior associate (she is next in line to become a partner if an opportunity comes up), she has general management responsibilities, in addition to client project management. She is responsible for supervising a team of architects, for recruiting new architects for the firm from people just graduating from architectural school, and for making sure all the office systems run smoothly. During the day, she may spend a good part of her time answering questions from architects on her team or mentoring young architects about how best to accomplish design projects. "A lot of what I do is show architects how to step back to see the bigger picture or zoom in to look at the details more closely."

Tonia enjoys working with younger architects, who often have new approaches to solving old problems. "I encourage them to question me. When I say we can't do it that way, I tell them, don't just accept that. Maybe you've got a good idea about how to do it." Tonia designed a whole new way to light baby nurseries when she was a young architect. "I didn't think about solving the problems the same way everybody had in the past. If I had known more about why it wasn't done that way, I might not have thought of a new solution, but because I didn't

> Who you work for early in your career, your mentor, can be one of the keys to your success.

have that knowledge, I was able to come up with a new way of doing it. People came from all over the country to see how we did it." In the system Tonia designed, a combination of florescent and incandescent lights are used so that the doctors and nurses can have just the right amount of light when needed, but the baby can sleep in darkness at other times. There is less danger of damaging the babies' eyes with this system.

Cuba, Bangkok, California, and New York

Tonia was born in Cuba, the daughter of a father who was in the U.S. military and a mother who was a teacher and then a substitute teacher. She and her older brother spent two years in Bangkok, Thailand, as young children. Then her family moved to California, where Tonia attended school up through the ninth grade.

Tonia showed her talents at a very young age. She was an excellent painter and had her own art show in Bangkok, just before the family left. "When we came back to the states, I took a few art classes, but I didn't like it. Everybody was expecting too much of me, and I wasn't doing it for myself anymore. So I quit between the seventh and eighth grade." In elementary school, Tonia built a scale model of the school. "I had trouble getting the flagpole the right length. I finally figured out how to measure the height by the shadow it cast."

In junior high Tonia took drafting courses. For a French class, she built a model of the Louvre, a famous art museum in Paris, France. Before her sophomore year, Tonia's family moved to New York. There Tonia took more drafting classes, and she built a model of a house she had designed for herself—a hexagon that was just tall enough for her. Her drafting teacher thought it was too unconventional, so he made her build a model of a more traditional house, using clay, balsa wood, and patterns of stone. "In high school I had taken most of the math and science classes already, so I worked on developing other skills, like interpersonal skills. I also swam and played intramural softball and soccer."

Architecture is a Team-Based Process

For college, Tonia chose the University of Texas at Austin. Her parents were from Texas originally, so she qualified for in-state tuition. Austin had an architectural program Tonia admired, and she fell in love with the city. Because she had graduated fourth in her high school class, she had no trouble getting into the program, a five-year course of study. In architecture school Tonia learned to think of a building as a series of spaces where people live or work. Then she learned how to create and build models fast, generating ideas to solve the architectural problems that presented themselves and then doing drawings to incorporate those ideas, and finally building the model to show the solutions.

Everyone in her class had to invent a client and build for that client. "I invented a cartoonist who did political satire. I had to design a house for this person. I'd have these conversations with the client in my head. That's when I realized that I like doing things that have constraints. The more constraints the better. It's the challenge of how to solve the problems that I really like."

"Architecture is about process more than learning to design a building. If your process is solid, your design will

GROUNDBREAKERS

A Remarkable California Architect

At her busiest in the 1920s, architect Julia Morgan (1872-1957) ran a business that employed 18 to 30 people in four offices and maintained an airplane and a pilot to transport her and her employees to various California construction sites.

Blonde, blue-eyed, and small, she was deceptively fragile looking, but contractors found they couldn't get shoddy work past her. She would climb ladders or crawl out on scaffold high above ground to inspect work.

One of California's "distinguished Bay traditionists," Julia's best known work was for William Randolph Hearst, famous newspaper publisher. She "collaborated" with Hearst for 28 years (1919-1937) to produce his fabled La Cuestra Encantada (now known as Hearst's castle) at San Simeon, California. From mountainside roads to guest houses, to the twin-towered castle of 100 rooms, she ran the entire project through her office.

Julia got her degree in civil engineering from the University of California in 1894, the second awarded a woman. She earned a degree from Paris's L'Ecole des Beaux-Arts in architecture in 1902, the first awarded to a woman.

be solid. Architects are like a conduit. You take in the information of what people want; overlay your expertise, your experience, and your creativity; and a design comes out the other side. It's a collaborative process; it's not just my building, it's the building my client wants. It's a totally team-based process. My school was very team-based so I learned how to work well as part of a team early on. Our workplace is totally team-based too. We've only succeeded when we're done if everyone feels they were an integral part of the output when a project is finished."

After architecture school Tonia went to work for a big architectural firm in Dallas called HDR that did a lot of institutional work, including hospitals. "Architecture is cyclical as a business. There are boom and bust times—except for health care, which is recession proof. Every time the system is changed, they have to build a new building to accommodate those changes."

Tonia was the only women in a firm of 200 architects. "I moved up very quickly. Part of it was my abilities and part of it was just that I got noticed. Being a woman in this industry has always either been a benefit to me or it hasn't been anything. Any time it's been an issue, it's been in my favor."

While she was working in Dallas, Tonia's parents had retired in Washington, D.C., where she landed a job with a small firm after spending two years with HDR. She found a great mentor in the owner and worked for that firm for six years. But the owner got sick and closed the firm, rather than selling it to his employees. Because Tonia didn't want to take clients from the firm while the owner was alive, she went to work for a year with a firm that oversaw the construction for Job Corps facilities nationwide for the U.S. Department of Labor. Her job was to assign the contracts to build the facilities and make sure the work

Architecture is process-based. You are moving through a series of constraints you have to solve.

was done right. After the owner of the firm died, she found a job at her present firm, where she has worked for nearly eight years.

Tonia is a sports nut. She plays golf and tennis, and she loves spectator sports. She also loves to travel. This year she went to Hawaii and the Bahamas. She is painting again, and she's thinking about the house she wants to design for herself.

Getting Started On Your Own Career Path

Getting Started On Your Own Career Path

WHAT TO DO NOW

To help you prepare for a career in construction, the women interviewed for this book recommend things you can do now, while still in school.

Colleen Lynch, Ironworker Apprentice

Get an erector set and explore how buildings and bridges are structured. If there are new buildings in your area, watch how they go up. Read about the history of construction, like how they built the Empire State Building or the Golden Gate Bridge. Sometimes television has programs on historic buildings.

Stay in math; there's a lot of math involved in ironwork.

Julie Odendahl, Electrician, Journeyman

Work on total fitness, especially upper body strength. Also work to make sure you develop good hand-eye coordination. Take lots of math classes, which you will need on the job, and science classes, which will help you understand electricity.

Get experience using power tools. If you want to get into an apprenticeship program, you have to know about the tools—how to use them safely. You may want to look for a volunteer project, such as Habitat for Humanity, where you can get experience using tools.

Before you choose a technical school, see if the local union accepts applicants from that school. Also make sure you understand the requirements for entering the union, and check more than once because they may change on a yearly basis.

Kristin A. Gunderson, Carpenter, Journeyman

Look for a summer camp that lets you do hands-on projects building or repairing things.

Habitat for Humanity may have a project in your area, go with a parent or other adult.

Check local efforts to fix up homes or build playgrounds. Many groups organizing these work days welcome volunteers of all ages.

Get a fix-it book and see if you can fix some things in your house.

Susan Byrd, Master Plumber

Every chance you get ask questions, and learn about tools and how to do things. If there is a Home Depot or similar store in your area, they may offer free classes to everyone and sometimes have classes just for kids.

Get your education and also learn how to read blueprints, either in high school or by reading books.

Margaret Nelson, Heavy Equipment Operator

Learn how to drive a stick shift. Keep physically fit.

Take math courses, because there is a lot of math involved in working heavy equipment. You need to know how to measure in feet, inches, widths, and lengths as you cut the road bed and follow instructions. You need to figure tonnage to order stone and asphalt.

Christine Keville

Work with your teachers to set up tours of construction sites. Invite construction and transportation officials to be guest speakers in your class.

Be involved in school clubs, associations, communities, church groups, and / or sports activities. You will develop the skills of leadership, organization, communication, and team-building, which are important in business and also may lead to scholarships.

Catherine Mahan, Landscape Architect

Most landscape architects are pretty nice people. We will take anybody in the door and show them what we are doing. Call one up and ask if you can visit to see what they do.

Get computer skills because a lot of design work is done on the computer using computer-assisted design (CAD) software. It's easier to communicate between firms, because the architect and the landscape architect can send emails in less time than sending paper documents back and forth. We also use other software to help convey what the job will look like.

If you are interested in a career that involves environmental landscape design, look for groups that need volunteers, like groups that clean up streams or work on trail maintenance.

Tonia Burnette, Architect

Build a model of your school or of something you love.

Take all the math and science you can. Also take drafting courses.

Recommended Reading

General References

Encyclopedia of Career and Vocational Guidance. (1997). Chicago: J. G. Ferguson Information Center

Peterson's Scholarships, Grants, and Prizes. (1997). Princeton, NJ: Peterson's. Web site: www.petersons.com

The Girls' Guide to Life How to Take Charge of the Issues that Affect You by Catherine Dee. (1997). Boston: Little, Brown & Co.
Celebrates achievements of girls and women, extensive resources

Training Centers, Trade Groups, and Construction Organizations

Many groups offer information on construction trades and encourage women to explore these trades through orientation programs. Some groups offer training classes. Some organizations serve as support networks for women. Listed below are some groups where you can start to explore career information. For additional organizations and unions, check your library or search the Internet. We recommend the www.Work4Women.org resource clearinghouse section. Viewers will be able to sort the list of organization, programs, and publications by type, population served (women vs. girls) and location by state.

Apprenticeship and Nontraditional Employment for Women (ANEW)
Renton Technical College
P.O. Box 2490, Renton, WA 98056
Phone: (425) 235-2212
ANEW offers free, 5-week training for construction and manufacturing careers with the average hourly wage of $11.00. Training components include carpentry, residential wiring, blueprint ready, sheet metal, ironwork, drywall, taping, painting, power and hand tool use, forklift driving, trades math, flaggers card, physical fitness, job and life skills, and job placement assistance. Trainees must be 22 years or older, reside in Seattle or King County, meet low-income guidelines and be motivated to work in physically strenuous jobs. GED, high school diploma, or any college studies are NOT required.

Arizona Women's Education and Employment (AWEE)
640 N. First Ave., Phoenix, AZ 85003-1515
Phone: (602) 223-4333
AWEE provides job-readiness training for unemployed and underemployed women and helps them find jobs and become economically self-sufficient.

Boston Tradeswomen's Network
62 Berkeley St., Boston, MA 02116
Phone: (617) 423-1535

Career Learning Center
1310 South Main Ave., Brookings, SD 57006
Phone: (605) 688-4370
CLC offers employment and training programs to unemployed or underemployed workers. The Center offers training for a variety of occupations including production welding and local and long-haul truck driving and career counseling to women working in nontraditional occupations.

Chicago Women in Trades
220 South Ashland Ave., Suite 101, Chicago, IL 60607-5308
Phone: (312) 942-1444; Web Site: womenintrades.org
A 16-year-old membership organization of women working in or seeking high-wage, blue-collar employment. Conducts advocacy, research, career awareness, and preparatory training to promote women's equal access and retention in male-dominated careers. Provides support services, counseling, and technical assistance. CWIT hosts Information Sessions for women to explore careers in the trades. Meets every Wednesday a.m. and in the evening of the 2nd Wednesday. Free.

Constructing Avenues Project–see Wider Opportunities for Women

Construction Management Association of America
7918 Jones Branch Dr., Ste. 540, McLean, VA 22102-3307
Phone: (703) 356-2622

Displaced Homemaker Program
Mt. Diablo Adult Education
1266 San Carlos Ave., Concord, CA 94518

Phone: (925) 685-7340 Web Site www.otan.dni.us/slrc/minigrant/diablo.html

Project Self-Sufficiency is a program for single parents and displaced homemakers to help them achieve economic self-sufficiency. The Nontraditional Employment for Women Project is a JTPA-funded program that helps women identify, enter, and complete job training leading to nontraditional employment.

Electric Women

2223 E Ocean Blvd., Long Beach, CA 90803

Phone: (310) 438-9493

IBEW union members reach out to support women's entry into the trades and to empower workers in general. Encourages diversity, democracy and solidarity within the union and the labor movement.

Electrical Training Trust (ETT)

515 South Ave. 19, Los Angeles, CA 90031-9990

Phone: (323) 221-5881; Web Site: www.companyinfo.com/ett

ETT offers vocational training for union construction electricians through apprenticeship and journey level programs in construction, electrical engineering, intercommunication sound and data, and transportation systems.

Employment Options, Inc.

101 E. Mifflin, Madison, WI 53704

Phone: (608) 244-5181

A non-profit women's career development center that offers a wide array of training and technical assistance services for women, employers, and labor organizations in construction, manufacturing, and technical fields.

Girls Count

225 E. 16th Ave. #475, Denver, CO 80203

Phone: (303) 832-6600; Web Site: www.girlscount.org

A nationally recognized non-profit organization working to ensure that today's girls are economically secure as adults. They believe this mission will be achieved by changing the systems affecting the expectations and achievements of girls, particularly in math, science, and technology; by conveying the importance of women's roles in the workforce; and by increasing the number of girls who understand the full spectrum of their life options and actively prepare for the future.

Girls Incorporated of Alemeda County

13666 East 14th St., San Leandro, CA 94578

Phone: (510) 357-5515; Email: ploomes@ousd.k12.ca.us

Girls, Inc. provides education, leadership, and career skills to girls and young women to help make them strong, bold, and smart.

Goodwill Industries of Atlanta

New Choices Program

2201 Glenwood Ave. SE, Atlanta, GA 30316-2399

Phone: (404) 486-8400; Web Site: www.goodwill.org/atlanta

New Choices Program helps persons experiencing barriers to employment to reach their fullest vocational potential. The program provides comprehensive vocational services and training. Services include career counseling and planning, vocational evaluations and assessments, case management, and work evaluations. The training programs provide pre-employment skill development and basic education/GED training through classroom and on-the-job instruction to prepare participants to work in nontraditional employment (Construction Trades for Women), custodial services, food service, hospitality services, self-employment.

Hard Hatted Women

4207 Lorain Ave., Cleveland, OH 44113

Phone: (216) 961-4449

Promotes the economic empowerment of women by preparing them for high wage careers in nontraditional occupations. Its programs include: (1) a skilled trades pre-apprenticeship training program, which prepares women for union apprenticeships and entry level nontraditional employment; (2) "Riveting News," a bimonthly newsletter about and for women in nontraditional jobs; (3) computerized job bank to match women looking for nontraditional jobs to employers seeking to hire women; (4) an annual career fair; and, (5) educational outreach through presentations and providing role models and mentors to students and interested women.

Indian Hills Community College

525 Grandview, Ottumwa, IA 52501-1398

Phone: (515) 683-5231; Web Site: www.ihcc.cc.ia.us/Conted/OtVoTech.htm

Encourages women and men to enroll in and successfully complete nontraditional training, and become employed. NEW (Nontraditional Employment for Women) is a 12-week pre-vocational workshop for women.

Institute for Women in Trades, Technology & Science (IWTTS)
3010 Wisconsin Ave. NW, Suite E-10; Washington, DC 20016-5052
Phone: (202) 686-7275; Web Site: www.serve.com/iwitts/
A nonprofit national organization dedicated to preparing women and girls for higher paying trades, technology, and science occupations; and preparing employers to successfully integrate women into their workforce.

International Union of Operating Engineers (IUOE)
National Training Program AFL-CIO
1125 17th St., NW, Washington, DC 20036
Phone: (202) 835-9679; Web Site: www.iuoe.org
Recruitment and training materials for women apprentices and journeywomen in heavy equipment construction. The IOUE is a progressive, diversified trade union which primarily represents Operating Engineers, who work as heavy equipment operators, mechanics, and surveyors in the construction industry, and Stationary Engineers, who work in operations and maintenance in building and industrial complexes, and in the service industries.

Louisiana Governor's Office of Women's Services
Training and Employment Center
2716-B Wooddale Blvd., Baton Rouge, LA 70805
Phone: (504) 922-2060
Free training and job placement assistance through building and industrial trade preparatory courses. Resource and referral center for dislocated workers and displaced homemakers.

Maine Tradeswomen Network
P.O. Box 10813, Portland, ME 04104
Phone: (207) 797-4801

Mi Casa Resource Center for Women, Inc.
571 Galapago St., Denver, CO 80204
Phone: (303) 573-1302; Web Site: www.micasadenver.org

A non-profit agency providing employment and education services that promote economic independence for low-income, primarily Hispanic women and youth. The Center provides computer training and employment training through the Avenidas (Avenues) project. Avenidas recruits, trains, and refers low-income women to nontraditional occupations. The 6-week training program focuses on skill development for highway and general construction jobs.

Michigan Tradeswomen
3815 Fort Street, Detroit, MI 48216
Phone: (313) 841-7380

Minnesota Women in the Trades
550 Rice St., St. Paul, MN 55103-2116
Phone: (651-228-9955

A nonprofit organization whose primary purpose is to help women find and keep well-paying jobs with good benefits in nontraditional occupations. WIT offers a 24-hour job hotline listing current openings, orientation sessions, a mentor program, and monthly social meetings. As part of WIT's outreach program, experienced tradeswomen volunteer to speak at various audiences to offer their insights into the day-to-day realities of their jobs.

Mission Valley Regional Occupational Program (MVOP)
40230 Laiolo Rd., Fremont, CA 94538
Phone: (510) 657-6124

MVOP provides vocational assessment, vocational training, case management, basic skills/GED, lifeskills classes, assistance with childcare and housing, referral services job development and job placement. Vocational training is available in women in the trades (carpentry and welding), medical assisting, network administration, computerized accounting, administrative support, and medical office management.

National Association of Home Builders
Women's Council
1201 15th St. NW, Washington, DC 20005-2800
Phone: (202) 822-0200; Web Site: www.nahb.com

The Women's Council represents more than 3,500 members who work in all aspects of the building industry—as owners, marketing experts, interior designers, and mortgage bankers. Members are employed by all types of industry-related businesses. The

Women's Council offers education, networking opportunities, publications, and other services to its members.

National Association of Women in Construction (NAWIC)
327 South Adams St., Fort Worth, TX 76104-1081
Phones: (800) 552-3506, (817) 877-5551; Web Site: www.nawic.org
NAWIC, an international association of women employed in the construction industry, promotes that industry and supports the advancement of women within it.

New Careers for Women
Community College of Rhode Island
400 East Ave., Warwick, RI 02886-1807
Phone: (401) 825-2300
NCW provides counseling on nontraditional educational opportunities, support services, and job placement assistance for women studying in the technical fields.

New Choices/New Options
YWCA City Center
704 State St., Erie, PA 16501
Phone: (814) 480-8792
Offers career preparation services for single parents, displaced homemakers, single pregnant women as well as individuals interested in nontraditional employment opportunities. Free programs are available in personal development, self-esteem building, career assessment and exploration, job readiness skills, basic computer and introduction to training in nontraditional work.

New Directions/ Career Services
Danville Area Community College
2000 East Main St., Danville, IL 61832
Phone: (217) 443-8597; Web Site: www.dacc.cc.il.us
Offers one-year certificate programs, two-year associate degrees, and some short-term training activities. It provides nontraditional career exploration, prevocational training in manufacturing, computer-aided drafting, electronics, power technology, welding, CDL trucking, computer networking, and criminal justice.

New York Tradeswomen
P.O. Box 870 Peck Slip Station, New York, NY 10272
Phone: (212) 227-2981

Nontraditional Employment Training
YWCA of Greater Milwaukee
3380 North 35th Street, Milwaukee, WI 53216
Phone: (414) 374-4460

Nontraditional Employment for Women (NEW)
243 W. 20th St., New York, NY 10011
Phone: (212) 627-6252

NEW prepares hundreds of women each year for work in the construction trades and other blue collar jobs through training, support services, and advocacy. It also assists women seeking advancement in nontraditional occupations. Training includes math, fitness, safety, job readiness, and basic skills in carpentry, electrical, and plumbing. Additionally, NEW provides technical assistance to employers and unions to create hostile-free work environments in order to improve the recruitment and retention of women.

Nontraditional Employment for Women–NY
243 W. 20th St., New York, NY 10011
Phone: (212) 627-6252

NEW helps low-income women become economically self-sufficient through employment in jobs which are nontraditional for women (women make up less than 25 percent of the labor force) with a focus on skilled, blue-collar trades that provide higher salaries and good benefits. NEW offers two 3-month training programs, New Blue and Blue Collar Prep, which combine literacy training and basic math with hands-on classes in woodshop, basic electricity, and physical fitness.

Northern New England Tradeswomen, Inc.
Step Up For Women
189 North Main St., Apartment #9, Barre, VT 05641
Phone: (800) 639-1472

NNETW provides comprehensive services for women working in or seeking to enter nontraditional employment. Step Up for Women, a 13-week skilled trades training program; Women Build, an on-the-job training program; and Employment Diversity in Highway Construction, a program using ISTEA half percent supportive service funds.

Oakland Women In Skilled Trades Program
Oakland Private Industry Council
1212 Broadway, Suite 300, Oakland, CA 94612

Phone: (510) 891-9393

A nationally recognized pre-apprenticeship training program that prepares women to enter the skilled trades and other blue collar occupations. In conjunction with a local community college, WIST provides training in the major construction trades, including carpentry, electricity, and plumbing.

Oceanside Single Parent/Homemaker
Oceanside Unified School District
2080 Mission Ave., Oceanside, CA 92054
Phone: (760) 967-1322
Offers mentoring, childcare, and transportation assistance to single parents and displaced homemakers.

Operating Engineers Women
335 Haddon Rd., Oakland, CA 94612
Phone: (510) 835-2511

Oregon Tradeswomen Network
P.O. Box 86620, Portland, OR 97286
Phone: (503) 281-0495
Web Site: tradeswomen.net
Dedicated to promoting success for women in the trades though education, leadership and mentoring.

Orientation to Nontraditional Occupational for Women (ONOW)
65 South Front Street, Columbus, OH 43215
Phone: (614) 466-5910
ONOW prepares women for nontraditional careers in manufacturing, construction, transportation, and high-tech industries in Ohio. This 8-week, 208 plus hours program currently operates at 11 sites statewide in vocational schools, community colleges, and correctional facilities. Over 90% of program graduates are placed into nontraditional training and/or employment annually.

Ozarks Technical Community College
New Perspectives
P.O. Box 5958, Springfield, MO 65801
Phone: (417) 895-7140

Career development program for single parents, displaced homemakers, and individuals entering occupations that are nontraditional for their gender. Financial aid and child care assistance is available.

Pre-Vocational Training Program
University of Iowa
C107 Seashore Hall Center, Iowa City, IA 52242-1402
Phone: (319) 335-0560
A free, 3-month training program (25 hours/week) to prepare women for construction, maintenance, repair, and technical occupations. Assistance with child care and transportation is provided. The training includes: (1) Physical Conditioning and Wellness, (2) Safety in the Workplace, (3) Career Development, (4) Life Skills, (5) Basic Technical Math and Measurement, and (6) Skilled Trade Shops and Other Nontraditional Opportunities. Students rotate through trade and technical shops at the university to become familiar with operations, shadow journey workers, and perform in a helper capacity.

Project for Homemakers in AZ Seeking Employment (PHASE)
University of Arizona
1230 North Park Ave., #209, Tucson, AZ 85721
Phone: (520) 621-3902
PHASE is a career-counseling program that assists single parents and displaced homemakers to enter training and find employment. Services include vocational counseling and testing, job search workshops, workshops for women (2-weeks) providing introduction to nontraditional occupations (NTO), scholarships available for specific NTO skills training and apprenticeship programs and small business development, skills training, and assistance with job placement and retention.

Project N.A.I.L., Arizona State AFL-CIO
(Nontraditional Assistance and Information Link)
5818 North 7th Street, #200, Phoenix, AZ 85012
Phone: (602) 631-4488

Professional Women in Construction
342 Madison Ave., Ste. 451. New York, NY 10173
Phone: (212) 687-0610

Rocky Mountain Tradeswomen's Network
PO Box 390617, Denver, CO 80239
Phone: (303) 429-5711

Sacramento Tradeswomen
1511 36th St., Sacramento, CA 95816
Phone: (916) 456-5555

San Francisco Women's Initiative for Self-Employment
450 Mission St., Suite 402, San Francisco, CA 94105
Phone: (415) 247-9473
A non-profit agency which offers bilingual business development training, consulting, and financing services designed specifically for low-income women. Their central goal is to assist women of diverse ethnic and social backgrounds to become self-sufficient through self-employment. Their programs link women with the resources they need to establish successful businesses with services designed to help them overcome the challenges they face along the way.

Solano Transition Services
Golden Hills Education Center
2460 Clay Bank Rd., Fairfield, CA 94533
Phone: (707) 421-6563
Focuses on nontraditional employment for women, career assessment and testing, job training, and placement services. School to career youth program.

STEP UP for Women–New Hampshire
17 Leavitt Lane, Durham, NH 03824
Phone: (603) 862-2996

STEP UP for Women–Vermont I
Room 32, City Hall, Burlington, VT 05401
Phone: (802) 865-7181

STEP UP for Women–Vermont II
P.O. Box 343, Ruthland, VT 05701
Phone: (802) 773-4881

Step-Up Program
Monongalia County Technical Education Center
1000 Mississippi St., Morgantown, WV 26505
Phone: (304) 291-9226

The Step-Up program is a tuition free, 11-week class designed to encourage and prepare women for entry level positions in (1) skilled trade occupations such as electrical, building construction, drywall, tile setting, labor, painting, etc., (2) technical areas like welding, auto mechanics, heating, ventilation and air conditioning, and drafting, and (3) public utilities, and building and grounds maintenance work.

Tools for Tomorrow: Women in the Trades
Madison Area Technical College
2125 Commercial Ave., Madison, WI 53704
Phone: (608) 246-5286

Helps women explore career options in construction, manufacturing, and technical occupations. Offers career exploration and pre-apprenticeship training classes in the evenings and on the weekends; job search counseling; and, "Tools for Change," a support group for tradeswomen and women interested in pursuing nontraditional occupations.

TOP-WIN, Inc. (Tradeswomen of Purpose/Women in Nontraditional Work)
2300 Alter St., Philadelphia, PA 19146
Phone: (215) 545-3700

Win is a non-profit organization made up of and representing women in nontraditional occupations. It focuses on increasing the number of women entering and remaining in blue collar nontraditional jobs in the Delaware Valley area.

Trades Mentor Network
2512 - 2nd Avenue # 209, Seattle, WA 98121
Phone: (206) 956-0703

Works with apprentices and mentors from five unions.

Tradeswomen, Inc.
P.O. Box 2622, Berkeley, CA 94702
Phone: (510) 487-6419

Wider Opportunities for Women
815 15th St., NW, Ste. 916, Washington DC 20005

Phone: (202) 638-3143; Web Site: www.w-o-w.org

Nationally, WOW uses its Web site to disseminate information and answer questions to increase the integration of girls and women in high-wage, nontraditional occupations. Work4Women (launch pending) will provide strategies, information and email listservs for women, girls, and workforce development professionals working on their behalf. In its Resource Clearinghouse section, viewers will be able to sort the list by type, population served and state location.

WOW's Constructing Avenues for Self-Sufficiency (204 Riggs Road, NE, Washington, DC 20002; Phone: (202) 526-7066) is a comprehensive program to assist Washington-area welfare recipients and non-custodial parents in building the skills necessary to enter apprenticeships and obtain jobs on highway and heavy construction projects in the metropolitan Washington region.

Women at Work

50 North Hill Ave., Suite 300, Pasadena, CA 91106

Phone: (626) 796-6870

A non-profit career and job resource center serving Southern California. Its mission is to help women reach their full employment and earning potential. Its services include job listings, career counseling, occupational testing, career exploration workshops, computer classes, nontraditional employment, and Latinas programs.

Women Construction Owners and Executives, USA

4849 Connecticut Ave., NW, Ste. 702, Washington, DC 20008

Phone: (202) 363-4822

Women Employed

22 West Monroe St., Suite 1400, Chicago, IL 60603

Phone: (312) 782-3902

A membership organization dedicated to expanding opportunities for women through career development services, education, and advocacy. Women Employed assists community colleges and nonprofit training institutions in developing pre-vocational training for women and girls. Its Career Links program, a group mentoring program linking teen girls with working women, focuses on life planning, career exploration, and job readiness activities.

Women In Construction Program
KY River Foothills Development Council
1623 Foxhaven Dr., P.O. Box 743, Richmond, KY 40476
Phone: (606) 624-2046
Training program which recruits and trains low-income women for jobs in construction. Program offers a combination of skills and life skill training.

Women In Nontraditional Occupations (WINTO)
P.O. Box 1075, New Haven, CT 06504
Phone: (203) 772-2710

Women In Nontraditional Employment Roles (WINTER)
1836 Nipmo Ave., Long Beach, CA 90815
Phone: (562) 570-3803
Provides technical assistance to unions, apprenticeship programs, and employers. Special areas and expertise include tradeswomen's issues, diversity, and design and implementation of nontraditional training programs for women.

Women in Skilled Trade
25 Selden SE #220, Grand Rapids, MI 49503
Phone: (616) 458-5443

Women in the Building Trades
555 Amory St., Jamaica Plain, MA 02130
Phone: (617) 524-3010
Women in the Building Trades promotes the entrance of women into blue-collar fields in an effort to help women earn higher pay and achieve economic viability. Three of their projects include: 1) the dissemination of information to women about jobs and training in the construction and technical trades; 2) courses which prepare women to enter the trades through acceptance into apprenticeship programs; and 3) "Introduction to the Trades for Young Women," which is directed at women ages 10-18.

Women in the Trades/Mission Valley ROP
40230 Laiola Dr., Fremont, CA 94538
Phone: (510) 656-0533

Women in Trades and Technology (WITT)
National Network

10 Douglas Court Unit 2, London, Ontario, N5W4A7 Canada
Phone: (519) 453-2105

Women in Transition
Mid-Plains Community College
1101 Halligan Drive, Voc-Tech Campus, North Platte, NE 69101
Phone: (308) 532-8740

Activities assist women to obtain marketable job skills through goal setting and removal of barriers to a positive change. Women are encouraged to choose nontraditional occupations or other high wage/high placement fields. Nontraditional training covers such options as auto mechanics, building construction and maintenance, diesel mechanics, drafting, electrical, electronics, and welding. Accompanying services are career assessment; basic skills review; workshops on building self-esteem, coping with divorce, and seeking a job; support services such as assistance with child care and transportation; and referral to community resources.

Women Unlimited
71 Winthrop St., Augusta, ME 04330
Phone: (800) 281-5259

A statewide organization providing trade and technical training and placement services to women wishing to pursue a nontraditional occupation. Services include 14-week training programs and a Job Bank connecting employers and tradeswomen.

Women Venture Construction Program
2324 University Ave. West, Suite 200, St. Paul, MN 55114
Phone: (612) 646-3808

Women Venture offers a comprehensive pre-apprenticeship program that places women into skilled trade positions. Since 1991, 284 women have successfully completed the training component and 71% of the graduates were employed in the trades and 37% in apprenticeships. The 5-week training and placement program addresses manual, personal empowerment, math, and job search skills, as well as job placement and support. Training content areas are carpentry, dry wall and taping, electrical, masonry, painting, plumbing, roofing, and tile setting. Also offers a 5-week printing program to prepare women to enter entry level jobs in printing industry with personal empowerment and self-esteem building and apprenticeship/internship at a printing company.

Women's Bureau, Region II
201 Varick St., Room 601, New York, NY 10014-4808
Phone: (212) 337-2389; Web Site: www.dol.gov/dol/wb (Click Regional Information)
A regional office of the Department of Labor's Women's Bureau that is the single unit at the Federal government level exclusively concerned with serving and promoting the interests of working women. In general, the Women's Bureau works to improve the economic status of all women by seeking equity in employment practices. More specifically, the Bureau is concerned about particular groups of women who have not been able to enter the work force because of difficulties in obtaining training, jobs, or advancement. Such difficulties may be related to age, sex, or race, or to social, economic, or geographic conditions.

Women's Bureau, Region IX
71 Stevenson St., Suite 927, San Francisco, CA 94105
Phone: (415) 975-4750; Web Site: www.dol.gov/dol/wb (Click Regional Information)
The Regional Women's Bureau office serves as the Labor Department's point of contact on the spectrum of issues affecting women in the workplace. It seeks to enlarge economic, civil and political rights, and opportunities for women through its educational and promotional activities, and technical and advisory services. It provides materials and services to agencies (public and private) whose scope of service varies (national to local).

Women's Development Center
Waukesha County Technical College
800 Main St., Pewaukee, WI 53072
Phone: (414) 691-5445
Helps people to help themselves. Through individual counseling and assistance, and career exploration and personal development classes, clients gain the knowledge and skills necessary to affect growth and change in their lives. Students are able to choose from a wide selection of offerings including nontraditional as well as traditional career exploration, interpersonal communications, aging issues, conflict resolution and job seeking skills. Many of these classes are free to displaced homemakers, single parents, single pregnant women, and women seeking high wage/high skill occupations.

Women's Employment Resource Corporation
3362 Adeline St., Berkeley, CA 94703
Phone: (510) 652-5484
Technical training for women ages 14 to 21; Job placement agency for all ages.

Women's Opportunity and Resource Development, Inc. (WORD)
127 North Higgins, 3rd Floor, Missoula, MT 59802
Phone: (406) 543-3550
A community-based, feminist organization that offers several projects to increase both women's self-sufficiency and sense of community with one another. Projects include Gearing Up, which offers building trades skills training to women interested in high-wage, nontraditional occupations.

Workables for Women
Route 30 West, Oak Valley, Clinton, PA 15206-0214
Phone: (800) 862-9317 (724) 899-3555

ARCHITECTS' ORGANIZATIONS

American Institute of Architects
also American Architectural Foundation
1735 New York Ave., NW, Washington, DC 20006
Phone: (202) 626-7300

American Society of Landscape Architects
636 Eye St., NW, Washington, DC 20001-3736
Phone: (202) 898-1185; Web Site:www.asla.org

OTHER

Habitat for Humanity
Look in your local phone book for a branch near you.

How COOL Are You?!

Cool girls like to DO things, not just sit around like couch potatoes. There are many things you can get involved in now to benefit your future. Some cool girls even know what careers they want (or think they want).

Not sure what you want to do? That's fine, too… the Cool Careers series can help you explore lots of careers with a number of great, easy to use tools! Learn where to go and to whom you should talk about different careers, as well as books to read and videos to see. Then, you're on the road to cool girl success!

Written especially for girls, this new series tells what it's like today for women in all types of jobs with special emphasis on nontraditional careers for women. The upbeat and informative pages provide answers to questions you want answered, such as:

- ✔ What jobs do women find meaningful?
- ✔ What do women succeed at today?
- ✔ How did they prepare for these jobs?
- ✔ How did they find their job?
- ✔ What are their lives like?
- ✔ How do I find out more about this type of work?

Each book profiles ten women who love their work. These women had dreams, but didn't always know what they wanted to be when they grew up. Zoologist Claudia Luke knew she wanted to work outdoors and that she was interested in animals, but she didn't even know what a zoologist was, much less what they did and how you got to be one. Elizabeth Gruben was going to be a lawyer until she discovered the world of Silicon Valley computers and started her own multimedia company. Mary Beth Quinn grew up in Stowe, Vermont, where she skied competitively and taught skiing. Now she runs a ski school at a Virginia ski resort. These three women's stories appear with others in a new series of career books for young readers.

The Cool Careers for Girls series encourages career exploration and broadens girls' career horizons. It shows girls what it takes to succeed, by providing easy-to-read information about careers that young girls may not have considered because they didn't know about them. They learn from women who are in today's workplace—women who know what it takes today to get the job.

EACH BOOK ALSO INCLUDES:

- ✔ A personality checklist for each job
- ✔ Lists of books to read and videos to see
- ✔ Salary information
- ✔ Supportive organizations to contact for scholarships, mentoring, or apprenticeship and intern programs

THE BOOKS ALSO LOOK AT:

- ✔ What skills are needed to succeed in each career
- ✔ The physical demands of the different jobs
- ✔ What the women earn
- ✔ How to judge whether you have the personality traits to succeed in the different jobs
- ✔ How much leisure time you'll have
- ✔ How women balance work and relationships
- ✔ Reasons for changing jobs
- ✔ The support received by women to pursue their goals
- ✔ How women handle pregnancy and child care
- ✔ What you need to study to get these jobs and others

So GET WITH IT! Start your Cool Careers for Girls library today...

ORDER FORM

Title	Paper	Cloth	Quantity
Cool Careers for Girls in Computers	$12.95	$19.95	_____
Cool Careers for Girls in Sports	$12.95	$19.95	_____
Cool Careers for Girls with Animals	$12.95	$19.95	_____
Cool Careers for Girls in Health	$12.95	$19.95	_____
Cool Careers for Girls in Engineering	$12.95	$19.95	_____
Cool Careers for Girls with Food	$12.95	$19.95	_____
		SUBTOTAL	_____

VA Residents add 4½ % sales tax _____
Shipping/handling $5.00+ $5.00
$1.50 for each additional book order (__ x $1.50) _____
                            TOTAL ENCLOSED _____

SHIP TO: (street address only for UPS or RPS delivery)
Name: _____
Address: _____

❏ I enclose check/money order for $____ made payable to Impact Publications
❏ Charge $____ to: ❏ Visa ❏ MasterCard ❏ AmEx ❏ Discover

Card #: _____ Expiration: _____
Signature: _____ Phone number: _____

Phone toll-free at 1-800/361-1055, or fax/mail/email your order to:
Impact Publications
9104 Manassas Drive, Suite N, Manassas Park, VA 20111-5211
Fax: 703/335-9486; email: orders@impactpublications.com